Education of the Gifted

Sunita Sharma

SHIPRA

Rs. 395, US$ 13

ISBN: 978-81-7541-296-5

2023 Impression, PoD
(2010, 2007, First Published in 2006)

Education of the Gifted

Published by:
SHIPRA PUBLICATIONS
LG 18-19, Pankaj Central Market,
I.P. Ext., Patparganj, Delhi 110092, India
Tel.: +91 11 22235152/6152, 9650028065
Email: info@shiprapublication.com
Website: www.shiprapublication.com

Preface

The group of gifted children is marginalized in Indian educational system and there is a huge wastage of their potential. These children do not get desirable attention in any sphere of life including education. The reason behind this is their advanced intellectual capacity for which they have to suffer by way of receiving unsuitable education. Most of the parents also do not know anything about giftedness. When they are told that their child is a gifted one, they don't understand what it means and what they should do.

Unawareness of our society about the potential and capabilities of these children takes them towards disappointment and frustration, and sometimes, towards suicide also. The need of the hour is to understand them. They need to be taught accordingly so that their potential can be harnessed. There is a wrong notion in our society that only the children who are deficient of some abilities, need extra attention so far as their education is concerned. This type of thinking is contrary to the current theories and quite damaging to the gifted children and the society at large. Educational system needs to be modified also according to the needs of the gifted as they have a different style of thinking, learning and working, because of their superior intellectual calibre. That is why educators have advocated for some reforms in the education system.

This book is quite comprehensive. It is my sincere hope that the book will be of immense value to the professionals in the field as well as to the parents. Though, I have tried my best to make the book as useful as possible, but readers are the best judge. I cordially invite the suggestions for improvement of the book for the benefit of parents, educators, researchers and other concerned people and ultimately, the gifted children.

Sunita Sharma

Contents

1

Intelligence and Problem Solving

Intelligence

Description and Significance

When issues related to giftedness are discussed, it becomes inevitable to understand the concept of intelligence. Right from the beginning, the meaning and the definition of the term intelligence has been perplexing the professionals of the field. Cicero introduced the term 'intelligentsia' which was supported by Burt (1955). Spearman (1927) remarked that the term intelligence was known in the fifteenth century, and that time, it was considered as a unitary trait. Burt (1955) held Spencer (1895) responsible for bringing the term intelligence in the field of psychology. Herbert Spencer was of the view that intelligence played a significant role in biology. It is the ability to adjust, as in the adjustment of men intelligence contributes a lot, while in lower animals instincts help them. He further defined the term as the power of combining many separate impressions. Spearman (1927) remarked that the term, became "only a vocal sound, a word with so many meanings that finally it had none". He quotes J.S. Mill's statement:

> "The tendency has always been strong to believe that whatever receives a name must be an entity of being, having an independent existence of its own. And if no real entity answering to the name could be found, men did not for that reason suppose that none existed, but imagined that it was something peculiarly abstruse and mysterious".

Guilford (1967) remarks that the term intelligence was defined after its tests had been constructed. Many definitions emerged but all were quite confusing and ambiguous to such an extent that professionals could not reach any conclusion.

Views of Alfred Binet

Although Binet constructed various tests to measure the intelligence but the literature reveals that he could not define the term with authenticity, however evidences are available that he used to express his views on the term during discussions. It is clear that he never agreed with British psychologists who emphasized on motor and sensory functions. He, in fact emphasized on imagery, memory, voluntary attention, common sense or judgment. Earlier, he considered judgment not different from resistance to suggestibility. But he withdrew this idea when it was clear to him that suggestibility was not possible with all children, *i.e.,* children with feeble mind or low intelligence. Later on he laid emphasis on some factors:

- *Direction*: This is now called mental set of the learner, *i.e.,* the learner's goal seeking activities.
- *Adaptation*: To choose the method or to find the techniques to reach the end.
- *Autocriticism*: This means self-judgment or evaluation.
- *Comprehension*: To comprehend the concept or idea.

All the four factors are included in present day definitions of intelligence. Binet did not accept the concept of one factor or monarchic theory of intelligence. He was of the view that intelligence is complex in nature and combination of different faculties which differ from each other. Binet (1909) states, "… the mental faculties of each subject are independent and unequal; with little memory there may be associated much judgment … Our mental tests, always special in their scope, are each appropriate to the analysis of a single faculty."

Functional Definition

A good definition should be precise, clear, unambiguous, practicable in nature and words used be explainable and definable. Wechsler (1958) to some extent has tried to fulfill these conditions while defining the term. He says that intelligence is the aggregate or global capacity of the individual to act purposefully, to think rationally, and to deal effectively with his environment. Wechsler's definition is comparatively more comprehensive and includes many aspects of intelligence. Although he has laid special emphasis on some words in the definition like aggregate, global, purposefully and rationally but he did not mention how or in what respect these words are more important or what these words include in them.

Another definition has been given by Boring (1923). He regards:

> "...intelligence as measurable capacity to do well in an intelligence test." He has described it in "Intelligence as the tests test it." The analysis of the definition leads us to conclude that intelligence is what intelligence tests measure. This makes it clear that intelligence tests were constructed before the definition of the term came into existence.

Apparently, the definition given by Boring seems to be quite vague and it was criticized also by some psychologists on the ground that it does not speak clearly anything about the term intelligence; rather for knowing intelligence tests, one has to understand what they are, what factors are measured or what factors they are based upon. This shows that in fact Boring wanted to raise the questions in the field of tests of intelligence.

Intelligence, Learning and Adaptation

Almost all the definitions of the term under discussion have a hidden idea that intelligence decides the learning capacity of an individual or the adaptation ability. On the other hand Binet has clarified that the child who obtains high scores is definitely intelligent and his learning capacity is no doubt quite good. But a child obtaining lesser score on the test proves that his learning ability is not so rapid or he may be slow learner. Husband (1939) explained learning ability as performance in learning tasks. To cut the story short, it can be said that the child's speed and amount of learning demands intelligence and it is the intelligence level that determines the quality of the learning trait of the child. Intelligence cannot be imagined unless factors included in it are known. Several tests are available but only one single test is never able to measure all the factors of intelligence. Suffice will be to say that there is no place for the word 'monolithic intelligence'. It is a well established fact that it is made up of a variety of factors. This is the reason why intra-individual differences in intelligence are found.

Intra-Individual Differences in Intelligence

Concept of uneven intelligence is as old as human beings. It is found in all individuals be it with average intelligence, mental retardation, giftedness or genius. Christal (1958) remarks that Binet and Henri (1896) had observed that children were unequally capable even within the limited areas of memory tests. Allowing for score reliabilities that were possibly not high, these observed intra-individual differences were apparently sufficient to lead those investigators to formulate hypotheses concerning five relatively independent memory abilities:

(*a*) Visual memory
(*b*) Memory for sentences
(*c*) Memory for musical tones
(*d*) Memory for colours
(*e*) Memory for digits

With the exception of memory for musical tones, the hypothesized abilities apparently resemble abilities differentiated by factor analysis.

Inclusion of all the factors in an intelligence test is must because one's intelligence cannot be described only on the basis of few factors. Each and every aspect of cognitive abilities has its own place in one's intelligence. The recently discovered aspect related to emotions has not been included in any of the intelligence tests. Sarason and Gladwin (1958), after reviewing numerous studies on sub-normality, had stressed the point that individuals who were mentally deficient, frequently made surprisingly good social and economic adjustments.

Intra-individual differences can very easily be seen among highly intelligent or even gifted population. Examples cited by Sandor (1932) are worth mentioning here. The examples are of one sided giftedness, one of whom was Polish, Dr. Finkelstein, who exhibited unusual accomplishments in numerical memory and numerical computations. He could memorize a matrix of numbers 5 × 5 in very short order and a list of 35 digits in one minute and yet he was only average in his ability to memorize visual figures. Among four such individuals, there was a difference in preferred mode of presentation of numbers for memorizing; some preferred visual presentation, and some auditory.

Some mentally retarded also show intra-individual differences in intelligence. They may have extraordinary ability in some areas. They are called 'idiot savants'. Scheerer, Rothmann and Goldstein (1945) have given the example of an eleven year old boy who stood very high in certain aspects and very low in others. He had good musical aptitude, remarkable memory for words and unusual numerical skills. On the other hand, he had little general information, missed social awareness and was generally low in verbal tests with intelligence quotient of 50.

Anastasi and Levee (1959) cite the example of a young man with an IQ of about 70 on either the Stanford-Binet or the Wechsler-Bellevue scale. He became an accomplished pianist and composer and was a good sight reader of music. He could recite two and half pages of prose after reading it once, but he could not report ideas from the passage. He did well in reciting lists of digits backward and remembered dates very well. He was especially poor in visual memory and in tests of induction and made a zero score on the Picture Arrangement Test. His verbal IQ was 92 but his performance IQ was 52 on the Wechsler scale.

Similarly, children with autism also sometimes show very good performance in certain areas of intelligence while in others they are retarded. Rimland (1964) observed that a certain small class of individuals, not recognized as idiot savants, is the autistic group, members of which are notoriously deficient in certain respects but exhibit island of even superior performance. Guilford (1967) opines that there is often especially good memory in some respects like for visual objects and for their arrangements in space. One child could reproduce a melody sung in a foreign language on hearing it once. There may be usually good musical talent, and the child may become expert at reading aloud, without comprehending anything read. Speech is acquired only in a parrot-like manner, not used as a means of communication. Almost all these drastic hiatuses in special abilities can be logically accounted for in terms of groups of primary mental abilities.

Hollingworth (1923) studied special strengths and weaknesses of children studying various school subjects. The special talents and weaknesses that she noted were observable by virtue of the fact that many children could have one of the talents alongside a weakness, such as being an excellent reader and a very poor speller, or within the subject of reading, being able to read the printed page fluently and yet not know what was said; or in arithmetic, being able to compute rapidly and accurately and yet be unable to solve arithmetic problems. Guilford (1967) has appreciated Hollingworth's work. He said that her book have been a gold mine of hypotheses for the factor analysts, had it been better known.

Latest Theories of Intelligence

Guilford's Model of Structure of Intellect

Guillford's structure of intellect is based on factor analysis. The model is the result of the problems of organizing the intellectual factors into a system. Almost forty such factors had been demonstrated (Guilford, 1956a; 1956b). In fact, the model was almost ready during nineteen fifties. But Guilford wanted to prepare a morphological model, *i.e.*, the model which could study the internal form of the words. He noticed the definitions of intelligence far from satisfactory. He said that intelligence comprises of 120 elementary mental abilities each of which involved the action of some operation upon some content to produce some product. Guilford was very much impressed by the theory of intelligence propounded by L.L. Thurstone who after factor analysis concluded about the primary mental abilities. Thurstone (1938) rejected all the previous theories of intelligence. His theory is called—Group Factor Structure of Intelligence. He analysed various factors separately and concluded that there are six Primary Mental Abilities (PMAs) which constitute human intelligence. They are:

(*i*) Verbal factor (V) shows the comprehension power of the individual.

(*ii*) Number factor (N) shows that how far the individual is good in numerical ability or counting or numerical calculations.

(*iii*) Word fluency (W) indicates how rapidly one can read and speak different words.

(*iv*) Space relations (S) show the spatial ability of the individual. This involves the ability in any task in which the individual manipulates an object imaginatively in space.

(*v*) Reasoning (R) factor decides the learner's ability to conclude, making rules or theories or principles, drawing inferences based on different instances.

(*vi*) Memory (M) factor reveals the ability to memorize the subject matters, incidences, situations, or ideas etc.

All the factors suggested by Thurstone are not independent. They are intercorrelated. Thurstone did not give any importance to the factor which is found in almost in all activities, *i.e.,* Spearman's 'g' factor.

Guilford (1967) proposed a three dimensional box like model in order to simplify the picture of intellectual traits' relationship. He was influenced by the researches conducted on the United States Air Force Personnel during World War II. It is in fact Guilford who for the first time took initiative to conduct systematic research in the field of intelligence. In his presidential address to the American Psychological Association in 1950, he presented his ideas on intelligence as well as creativity. He is of the view that although each factor is sufficiently distinct to be detected by factor analysis, but now it has become apparent that the factors themselves can be classified because they resemble one another in certain ways.

One basis of classification is according to the basic kind of process or operation performed. This kind of classification gives us five major groups of mental abilities:

(*a*) Cognition
(*b*) Memory
(*c*) Convergent production
(*d*) Divergent production
(*e*) Evaluation

Guilford defines cognition as discovery or re-discovery or recognition. Memory means retention of what is cognised. Two kinds of productive thinking operations generate new information from known information and remembered information. In divergent thinking operations the individual thinks in different directions, sometimes searching, sometimes seeking variety. In convergent thinking the information leads to one right answer or to a recognised best or conventional answer. In evaluation, one reaches to decisions as to goodness, correctness, suitability or adequacy of what one knows, what one remembers and what one produces in productive thinking.

A second way of classifying the intellectual factors is according to the kind of material or content involved. The factors known thus involve four kinds of material or content:

(*a*) Figural
(*b*) Symbolic
(*c*) Semantic
(*d*) Behavioural

Figural content is concrete material that is perceived through the senses. It does not represent anything except itself. Visual material has properties such as size, form, colour, location or texture. Things one hears or feels provide other examples of figural material. Symbolic content is composed of letters, digits and other conventional signs, usually organised in general systems such as the alphabet or the number system. Semantic content is the form of verbal meanings or ideas.

In the beginning Guilford talked only about three types of contents but he added one more category of content when previous three were supported by the professionals. Guilford (1958a) observes that this step was taken on purely logical grounds, for there were no known factors at the time to support the idea. The kind of content, called by the term 'Behavioural' was added to take care of the kind of information involved in cognition and in other operations pertaining to the behaviour of other people. Further, he said that we know to some extent what the other person is perceiving, attending to, feeling, thinking and intending to do. Inferences are drawn from this information and such information are utilised in efforts to control one's actions.

The product dimension was thought to be included more slowly. Guilford (1967) remarks that it came about because of the need for taking into account the parallels that appeared across both the content and the operation categories. That is, if we take a set of factors having in common one of the content properties, say semantic, and also one of the operation categories, say cognition, we have a set of semantic cognition abilities, not just one. There are parallels to these abilities if we change either to a new content category, say divergent production, or to a new combination of both content and operation, such as figural – divergent – production abilities.

When a certain operation is applied to a certain kind of content, as many as six general kind of products may be involved. There is enough evidence available to suggest that regardless of the combinations of operations and content, the same six kinds of products may be found associated. The six kinds of products are:

(*a*) Units
(*b*) Classes
(*c*) Relations
(*d*) Systems
(*e*) Transformation
(*f*) Implications

The factor analysis revealed that these are the only fundamental kinds of products that one can know. As such they may serve as basic classes into which one might fit all kinds of information psychologically.

For explaining these three kinds of classifications of the factors of intellect, Guilford prepared a single solid model called "Structure of Intellect."

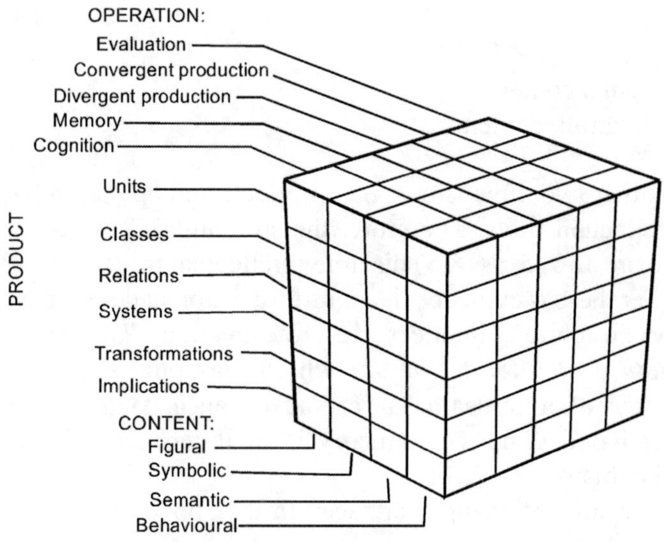

The model depicts that there are 120 (5 × 6 × 4) discrete intellectual traits or mental abilities, which explain the term intelligence in a comprehensive fashion.

On the other hand, the following model reveals, some differences in the factors:

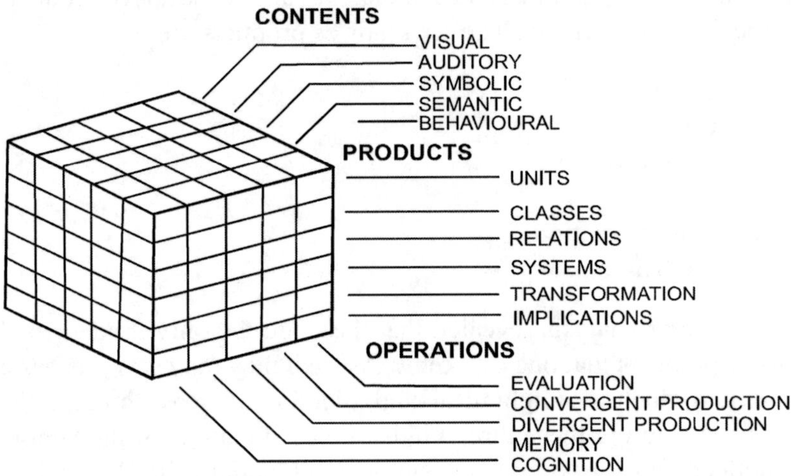

The above model shows that the figural content is divided into two parts:

- Visual contents
- Auditory contents

The other two dimensions, *i.e.,* products and operation have the same intellectual traits. Therefore, the structure of intellect reveals that there are 150 (5 × 6 × 5) discrete intellectual traits.

Further there is evidence that Guilford again made some changes in his own structure of intellect. He wrote an article *Some changes in the structure of intellect model* which was published in 1988, unfortunately after his death. The article reveals that Guilford himself was not satisfied with his own theory of intelligence. He changed the model like this:

Two prominent changes are seen in the above model. The first change involves the separation of figural content column into visual and auditory categories. The two categories were previously combined because of very limited number of auditory factorial abilities that had been reported. The second change that occurred in the revised structure of intellect is a new column, *i.e.,* memory retention and the former memory column has been renamed as 'memory recording' in the model. The 'memory recording' column involves short-term memory. Thus, finally there are 180 (5 × 6 × 6) discrete intellectual traits or mental abilities in an individual according to Guilford (1988).

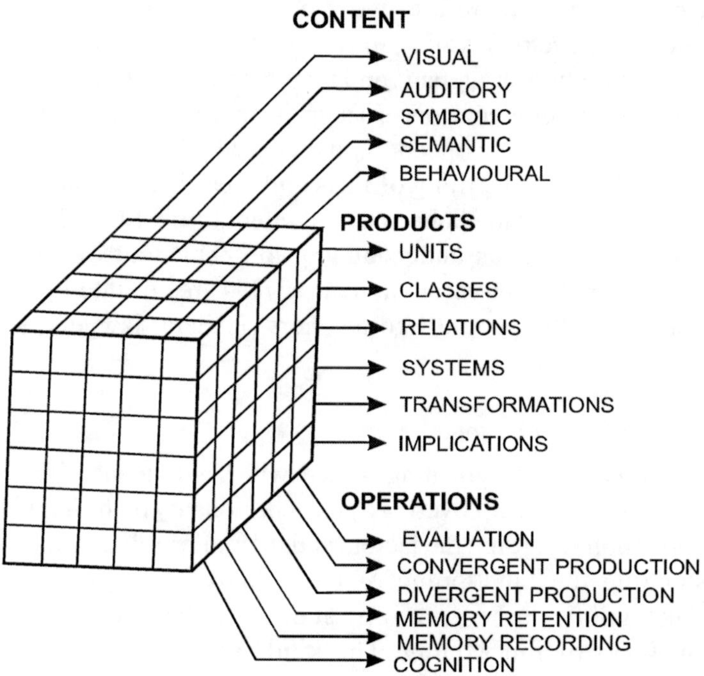

Implications of the Structure of Intellect

The utility of the SOI is in three areas:

In the Field of Vocational Testing

The structure of intellect is a theoretical model that predicts many distinct abilities, if every cell of the model contains a factor. Many of the factors are inter-correlated; so, by appropriate sampling it is possible to cover the important abilities with a more limited number of tests. At any rate, a multiple-score approach to the assessment of intelligence is definitely indicated in connection with future vocational operations.

In the content part, mainly there are four types of intelligences. The abilities involving the use of figural information may be regarded as concrete intelligence. Operators of machines, engineers, musicians, artists etc. mostly depend on this type of intelligence as they deal with concrete things and their properties. In the symbolic and semantic cell of content part, there are two types of abstract intelligences. Symbolic ability helps learning to recognize words, to spell, and to operate with numbers. Language and mathematics depend much upon them. Semantic intelligence plays a significant role for understanding things in terms of verbal concepts and that is why it is important in all the courses where the learning of facts and ideas is necessary.

Guilford justifies the behavioural content of the SOI. He calls it as social intelligence, as understanding the behaviour of others or ourselves is largely non-verbal in nature. This area of intelligence is more useful for the people like teachers, leaders, lawyers, social activists, therapists etc.

In the Field of Psychology

Factor analysis helps investigating ways in which individuals differ from each other, *i.e.,* it helps discovering traits of personality of the individual. The information regarding the factors and their inter-relationship helps understanding the functioning of individuals. Different kinds of intellectual abilities in terms of operations may be said to represent different ways of functioning. The kinds of intellectual abilities distinguished according to varieties of test content and the kinds of abilities distinguished according to varieties of products suggest a classification of basic forms of knowledge or information. The concepts provided by the distinctions among the intellectual abilities and by their classifications may be very useful in researches in the field of learning, memory, problem solving, invention and decision making by any method chosen to approach those problems.

In the Field of Education

Regarding educational utility Guilford remarks that the most fundamental implication is that we might well undergo transformation with respect to our conception of the learner and of the process of learning. The learner is a kind of stimulus response device, much on the order of a vending machine. He says that you put a coin and something comes out. The machine learns what reaction to put out when a certain coin is put in. If, instead, we think of the learner as an agent for dealing with information, where information is defined very broadly, we have something more analogous to an electronic computer. We feed a computer information, it stores that information; it uses that information for generating new information either by way of divergent or convergent thinking; and it evaluates its own results. Advantages that a human learner has over a computer include the step of seeking and discovering new information from sources outside itself and the step of programming itself. Perhaps even these steps will be added to computers, if this has not already been done in some cases.

Education is not a matter of training the mind or training the intellect. In theory, the emphasis has been upon the learning of rather specific habits or skills. If cue from factor theory is taken, it is recognized that most learning probably has both specific and general aspects of components. The general aspect may be along the lines of the factors of intellect. This is not to say that the individual's status in each factor is entirely determined by learning. It is not known that to what extent each factor is determined by heredity and to what extent by learning. The best position for educators to take is that possibly every intellectual factor can be developed in individual at least to some extent by learning.

No doubt that education has the general objective of developing the intellect of learners, it can be said that each factor of the intellect provides a particular goal. Defined by a certain combination of content, operation and product, each goal ability then calls for certain kinds of practice in order to achieve improvement in it. This implies the choice of curriculum and the choice or innovation of teaching methods that will most likely accomplish the desired results.

The detailed factorial analysis of a variety of factors reveals that it is now possible to know whether any general intellectual skills are being neglected in education and whether appropriate balance is being observed. Guilford emphasises more on training in divergent thinking area as compared with training in convergent thinking, evaluation or critical thinking or judgement ability

Some more models of intelligence have emerged during recent years.

Perkins' Model

Perkins in 1995 observed that intelligence includes:

- Neural intelligence
- Experiential intelligence
- Reflective intelligence

Sternberg's Triarchich Theory of Intelligence

Sternberg (2000) has explained the phenomenon of intelligence in a different fashion. A model has been developed called 'triarchic' theory of intelligence. It consists of:

- A contextual sub-theory, that refers to the intelligence to the external world of the individual.
- A two-facet experiential sub-theory that refers to the intelligence to both the internal and external world of the individual.
- A componential sub-theory, which refers to the intelligence to the internal world of the individual.

Sternberg remarks that his triarchic theory of intelligence features the executive and control functions of intelligence – the decision making functions of intelligence that have not been well addressed by past intelligence tests by Terman and Wechsler.

Neisser (1979) has very aptly remarked that a single definition cannot be used to explain this multifaced phenomenon as there are many kinds of intelligences now. An alternative view to the traditional conception of intelligence has been put forth by the neuropsychologist Howard Gardner.

Theory of Multiple Intelligences

It looks at human potential in its broadest sense. Gardner (1983) defines 'intelligence' as a "biopsychological potential to process information that can be activated in a cultural setting to solve problems or create products that are of value in a culture."

Gardner has broadened the scope of 'intelligence'. He has pluralized the term and observed that separate faculties for dealing with different kinds of symbol systems have been given to us. He collected evidences from electric sources, including neuropsychology, developmental and experimental psychology and concluded that there are eight types of intelligences which are as follows:

Multiple Intelligences

Intelligence	*End Ït tes*	*Core Components*
Logical-mathematical	Scientist, mathematician	Sensitivity to, and capacity to discern, logical or numerical patterns; ability to handle long chains of reasoning.
Linguistic	Poet, Journalist	Sensitivity to the sounds, rhythms, and meanings of words; sensitivity to the different functions of language.
Musical	Composer, violinist	Abilities to produce and appreciate rhythm, pitch and timbre; appreciation of the forms of musical expressiveness.
Spatial	Navigator, Sculptor	Capacities to perceive the visual-spatial world accurately and to perform transformation on one's initial perceptions.
Bodily-Kinesthetic	Dancer, Athlete	Abilities to control one's body movements and to handle objects skilfully.
Inter-personal	Therapist, Salesman	Capacities to discern and respond appropriately to the moods, temperaments, motivations and desires of other people.
Intra-personal	Person with detailed, accurate self-knowledge	Access to one's own feelings and the ability to discriminate among them and draw upon them to guide behaviour; knowledge of one's own strengths, weaknesses, desires, and intelligences.

Apart from all these, Gardner has also added one more intelligence, *i.e.,* naturalist intelligence.

The academic success depends on linguistic and logical-mathematical intelligences. In fact these two are traditional intelligences. But Gardner says that individuals who are proficient in other areas like performing art, *i.e.,* dance or music are also intelligent. Further, Gardner lays emphasis on the important role of socio-cultural factors in the development of different intelligences. A child should be provided with the opportunities for cultivation of any particular type of intelligence.

Implications of the Theory of Multiple Intelligences

The teachers need not to emphasise too much on traditional intelligence, *i.e.,* linguistic and logical-mathematical only. The child can do better in other areas also as there exist other intelligences. Gardner has used electric sources of data while formulating his theory. This throws light on the nature of intelligences and their assessment. Intelligence is complex, and a number of tasks in appropriate context are required to assess it. Plain paper and pencil tasks will not do. Educators need to know that traditional tests of intelligence can not reveal the potentials of the child. Gardner has indicated the shortcomings of standardized tests. Moreover, he is suspicious also about the theory's application in schools as he says that teachers may misunderstand the theory. In fact Gardener has not offered concrete application criteria and leaves it to the educators to develop for themselves (Sankaranarayanan, 2003). He is not in favour of labelling children on the basis of particular types of intelligences. But he is sure that the multiple intelligences concept has diversified the differentiated lessons provided to gifted students (Ramos – Ford and Gardner, 1997).

Emotional Intelligence

Aristotle has said that it is easy to show anger. But to be angry with right person, to the right degree, at the right time, for the right purpose and in the right way is not easy.

This leads us to the education of emotions. Every individual has two minds:

- Emotional mind
- Rational mind

In 1920 E.L. Thorndike had propounded the term 'Social Intelligence'. Emotional intelligence is not different from social intelligence. The term emotional intelligence was first introduced by a graduate student of U.S.A. while writing a doctoral dissertation in 1985. Two American psychologists, Peter Salovey from Yale and John Mayer from the University of Hampshire summed up some qualities of human beings in the late 1980s. The qualities were: empathy, self awareness, emotional control etc. In 1995, Daniel Goleman of New York Times adopted it and wrote a book *Emotional Intelligence*. He gave the word a new meaning. According to Goleman intelligence quotient accounts for only 20 per cent of a person's success in life. Balance can be attributed to emotional intelligence or EQ. The word EQ is used interchangeably with Emotional Intelligence. This refers to emotional awareness and emotional management skills which provide the ability to balance emotions to reach the maximum level of happiness. People with low EQ are misfit in the social set up.

Hein (2004) defines emotional intelligence as the mental ability we are born with, which gives us our emotional sensitivity and our potential for emotional learning management skills and which can help us maximize our long term health, happiness and survival. Mayer, Salovey and Caruso define it as the ability to process emotional information, particularly as it involves the perception, assimilation, understanding and management of emotion. They further observe that emotional intelligence consists of "four branches of mental ability:"

- Emotional identification, perception and expression
- Emotional facilitation of thought
- Emotional understanding
- Emotional management

EQ is largely learnt and continues to develop throughout the life. It is not genetically fixed rather it can be improved. An individual can acquire emotional competencies which may lead him to outstanding performance. Development of EQ helps him in gaining happiness, adjustment, health, success in life and relationship with others. It helps also in taking decisions and solving problems.

Hein has given some suggestions for developing emotional intelligence:

- Label your feelings, rather than labelling people or situations.
- Distinguish between thoughts and feelings.
- Take more responsibility for your feelings.
- Use your feelings to help them make decisions.
- Show respect for other people's feelings.
- Feel energised, not angry.
- Validate other people's feelings.
- Practice getting a positive value from your emotions.
- Don't advise, command, control, criticise, judge or lecture to others.
- Avoid people who invalidate you.

Hein appreciates Goleman for highlighting the importance of emotions and emotional intelligence in the life of a person. But Hein on the other hand has felt that Goleman has misled the public also to some extent. Some points of criticism of Goleman's views have been presented by Hein. They are:

- He makes unsupported claims about the power and predictive ability of emotional intelligence.
- His own, self-created definition of emotional intelligence includes aspects of personality and behaviour which are not correlated to emotional intelligence as it is scientifically defined. He also interchanges terms such as emotional literacy, emotional health, emotional skills, and emotional competency. He never defines any of these other terms, but he equates them all to emotional intelligence.
- He tries to make us believe he is presenting something new, when in fact much of what he is reporting has been studied for years under personality research.
- He implies that anyone can learn emotional intelligence and fails to acknowledge either the relatively fixed nature of the personality traits he includes in his definition of EI or the differences in innate potential among individuals.
- He presents himself as the sole expert in emotional intelligence and fails to give adequate credit to Mayer, Salovey, Caruso and others.

- He represents his work as "Scientific" when it does not hold up to scientific scrutiny.
- His personal beliefs about what is "appropriate" contradict the academic theory concerning the value of our emotions. He still seems to regard emotions as largely something to be controlled and restrained, rather than something to be valued.

Problem Solving

It is the problem that presents challenges before an individual. People with more responsibilities have to face more problems. In our country, challenging educational problems are presented before students very rarely. Most of the time the students, solve the problems following the already set methods. Problems in the field of education should be of such type that they can compel the child to utilise the cognitive abilities. Such type of problems or challenges can help the child to think deeply for getting the solution. As a noun the word 'problem' means any situation which has no immediate solution. It is any trouble, difficulty, vexed questions, mess, dilemma or complication. Davis (1973) defines the term like this:

> "A problem is a stimulus for which an organism does not have a ready response."

When one is able to solve a problem and gets its solution, it does not remain the problem anymore as the solution has come out. Problem solving is about as broad as behaviour of an individual. A problem can never be solved in a haphazard fashion. It involves a certain sequence.

Sequence of Steps in Problem Solving

The literature reveals that many professionals of the area have proposed the steps of problem solving. Dewey (1910) divided all the steps into five categories which are as follows:

- The first step of solving any problem is feeling of a difficulty, trouble, confusion or any doubt. The individual is not clear to choose the way where he should go, *i.e.,* how to come out of that complicated situation.

- Second step is of defining the typical situation, *i.e.,* the individual tries to know the situation in a real sense.
- When the problem is clearly in the knowledge of the individual, different methods or techniques of the solution are found out. Many remedies come in the mind in the form of suggestions. In other words, the individual thinks about many answers which may help him in solving the problem.
- At fourth stage the learner is conspicuous about the results or consequences of the solutions which come in his mind, *i.e.,* he thinks about the net result of the use of a particular method or technique.
- In the end, the final method chosen is applied to remove the difficulty and the individual is out of the complicated situation. At this stage the learner is quite clear about the way of answering and getting the right response.

It will not be out of place to mention here that all the steps are not followed always very strictly. Some modifications and changes also have their place. Sometimes the learner may skip first, second and even third step and directly come to the fourth and fifth steps. This depends on the cognitive abilities of the learner. However, Dewey's stages of problem solving have not been able to receive much attention, but their utility with practicability cannot be denied. Moreover, divergent thinking has not got sufficient space as only the stage third, *i.e.,* when the individual thinks in a diversified manner to get the real solution is seen as creative potential, otherwise all the steps involve convergent thinking.

Johnson (1955) has opined that three steps are involved in problem solving:

- Preparation
- Production
- Judgement

Merrifield *et al.* (1962) suggest five steps in the process of problem solving. They are:

- Preparation
- Analysis
- Production
- Verification
- Reapplication

All these five steps are not much different from those proposed by Dewey.

Walls (1926) has opined that there are certain stages involved in problem solving. Details of which are as follows:

(a) Preparation

In the beginning, the individual prepares himself for dealing with the complicated situation. He studies thoroughly the whole situation. Preparation involves some phases like:

(*a*) Thorough knowledge of the matter concerned.
(*b*) The individual intends to get the solution of the problem.
(*c*) The felt need leads the learner to find out the way through which he can solve the puzzle or difficult situation. This is called searching stage.

(b) Incubation and Illumination

The word incubate means to hatch or to brood. It is quite obvious that the thought in the shape of a problem in the mind of an individual is for sometime in incubation, *i.e.,* in the hatching process. This may be called as illumination also. The term illumination is quite surprising to most of the professionals as it seems as the most strange or dramatic aspect of creative production. Westcott (1961) defines the term as "intuitive leap." This also tells us that a sudden leap in thoughts or ideas is illumination.

Guilford (1967) says that incubation is a period during which there is no apparent activity by the individual for solving the problem but during which and at the end of which there is often evidence of material progress toward a solution. Further he explains that the period of incubation may be a matter of minutes, days, months and even years. During incubation, the problem is there in the mind but apparently the individual may be busy in some other activities. The thought remains under problem solving process. Then suddenly an idea comes in the mind and the person finds the solution. The stage of incubation has been very important for the professionals.

Olton (1979) expresses that incubation is a facilitation of thinking (not simply of recall) that is evident after an interval during which no conscious work was done on the task assuming an earlier period of substantial conscious work. It is not a readymade answer. Khatena (1982) defined it as

> "... that stage in creative thinking and problem solving when mental events, earlier set in motion by deliberate and intensive preparation, are energised to become autonomous for the occurrence of fruitful insights that lead good solutions of problems."

It is important to note that for the first time it was said that incubation as a process becomes autonomous. Autonomy here means that the individual is not always conscious and bothered for the answer. The answer comes in the mind freely. Poincare (1913) has stated that during incubation unconscious problem solving goes on. On this view, Guilford (1967) remarked that this hypothesis tells us practically nothing, of course. He further says that still it is not clear what the unconscious psychological operations are, if nothing more is said.

Wallas (1926) has added the term intimation which exists between incubation and illumination. It emerges just before illumination. The individual becomes conscious that something is going to happen (Tripathi, 1996). Wallas says that this very consciousness is called intimation, and if intimation is allowed to mature sufficiently, there is likelihood that it will result in illumination. Incubation does not take place only in educational problems' solution rather it takes place in solving the problems of general life also.

Fulgosi and Guilford (1970) conducted a study to find out the effects of incubation on divergent thinking which helps a lot in problem solving and creative potential. A total time of four minutes was given for two questions requiring divergent thinking:

- What would be the results if everyone suddenly lost ability to read and write?
- What would be the results if none of us needed food anymore in order to live?

The subjects under study were asked to give as many consequences as they could think of in a given period. One group of subjects worked continuously for four minutes on the items. A second group worked for two minutes on the task, worked for ten minutes on an unrelated task, and worked again for final two minutes on the task. A third group worked on the test for two minutes, then spent twenty minutes on a test on an unrelated task, returning to the original task for final two minutes. The results of the study revealed that the group which got twenty minutes for incubation did better in terms of quantity of responses, *i.e.,* fluency, while the ten minutes interval group gave more original responses.

But this research work has been criticised by Olton (1979) by reporting that when Silveria replicated the above mentioned study, the results were quite different. She could not find and confirm the positive effects of incubation as revealed by Fulgosi and Guilford (1970). Olton further remarks that the experimental situation was artificial and lacked motivational thrust that a real life situation will have. Besides, the problems given to subjects were mere puzzles or insight problems. These would hardly arouse any kind of motivation that a research worker will be having while fully engrossed in a problem.

Trying to remove all the above mentioned limitations, Olton (1979) conducted an experiment in which incubation was studied under more realistic situations. For the experiment, experienced chess players were given a challenging problem from chess which could be worked out individually. Such problems are known as end-game study. The subjects in the incubation group were instructed to "take a break" at some point of their choosing around the end of first hour of their work on the task. The break consisted of a two hour period during which they could eat lunch, browse through books, loaf around etc., they were not to think about chess. The experimental situation was very much like the real life situation. The period of incubation appeared to help in the solution of the problem and fifty per cent of the experimental group was able to come to the correct solution. When compared with the control group, it was found that there too fifty per cent were able to solve the problem. The experimental group failed to show any superiority. A final analysis in terms of moves and sequences was made but it too failed to show any superiority in the experimental group.

Patrick (1935, 1938) selected the subjects working on poems or scientific problems in the laboratory. Periods of incubation occurred when an individual dropped one idea or strategy for a time and returned to it later. There was not complete cessation of problem solving effort in these instances but such pauses might be in somewhat the same category. Better examples were obtained when Patrick had half of the subjects planning experiments in the laboratory and the other half at home, with lapsed time for incubation. The investigator concluded that the group with the incubation period produced somewhat better ideas. Though it was quite risky that subjects might have lost control over conditions of work.

Exacerbation of Incubation and Illumination

Incubation takes place itself and automatically. The individual needs to be not in mental pressure. Mental freedom and relaxation are most necessary for it. No compulsion and intentional efforts help in this process. Problem solving or creativity sometimes may take no time and at times much time. The individual should be given the time for mental relaxation as problem solving and creativity need not to be considered as time bound activities. Suddenly the idea may come in the mind even while one is simply walking as during this time the individual is not involved in any other activity. That is why the brain works for thinking and without efforts the desired idea can emerge and problem can be solved. Olton (1979) has observed that walking is a non-focal activity and does not require any attention. Mind, therefore, is in a relaxed state which may be helpful for the generation of new ideas. Besides, the individual may be asked for changing the medium of thinking such as from verbal thinking to thinking with the help of images. This may help to generate the ideas. Active reading, *i.e.,* creative reading leads for spontaneous answer.

(c) Verification

Verification refers to confirmation and authentication of the solution. This step takes place at the end of problem solving. The person, after crossing all the steps, tries to know that whatever the results have come out whether they are right or wrong.

The discussion in previous pages makes it clear that problem solving is linked with creativity. It is an intellectual activity. There is something creative about all genuine problem solving, and creative production is typically carried out as a means to the end of solving some problem (Guilford, 1967). Further Guilford says that creativity and problem solving entail transfer recall; if only replicative recall were involved, there would be no problem solving and nothing creative about the behavioural event. The components of both the processes are common.

2

Giftedness

Nature and Significance

Right from the beginning, professionals have not been one on the question of definition of giftedness. Abraham (1958) has reported that one of his students had presented one hundred and thirteen definitions of the term giftedness while preparing his term paper. This indicates the lack of uniformity on the definition of mentally superior children. The most common method used to define the term is the scores obtained by the individual on any intelligence test. It is worth mentioning here, that the term intelligence has also been controversial. Some are of the view that the IQ score differs if the test has been given individually or in a group. Moreover, the professionals have not used the same intelligence test, hence the scores may differ. Terman *et. al.* (1925) used only intelligence scores for identifying gifted children. The criterion of selecting gifted for his longitudinal study was only IQ. Hollingworth (1931) also observed that high IQ was the only way to identify gifted children with certainty, however, she could not save herself from criticism.

The use of IQ test has its own objectivity as it can be measured even at an early age, *i.e.,* childhood. But on the other hand it is also possible that children coming from low socio-economic strata may not score as high because they cannot perform on verbal tests properly. They may show their high ability in later years in the form of an artist, musician, leader, social activist etc. Hence, need was felt to broaden the definition of giftedness so that talent, aptitude and other traits could also be included (Witty, 1958). No doubt, intelligence is the basic component of giftedness. But Terman's view is narrow in the sense that he takes the intelligence as fixed and decided by heredity.

Sternberg (1985) has very aptly remarked that an IQ score provides too narrow a view of individuals and their capabilities and therefore does not accurately represent an individual's capacity to learn and achieve. Now the idea about the concept has changed. Researchers now believe that intelligence is not determined only by heredity rather environment also plays its role in it, *i.e.,* it can be diminished or enhanced also. But they do not speak of contribution of Terman in the field of giftedness.

Galton (1869) studied giftedness in a scientific fashion. His studies revealed that people's natural abilities were derived from inheritance in much the same way as did such features as height and other physical attributes. He studied the biographies of individuals with outstanding achievements. On the basis of these researches, he concluded that the principal elements which contributed a lot to their achievement were "ability, zeal, and readiness to work." Galton felt that each of these was in part a result of inheritance, but that the most important factor was the "gift of high ability." These studies led him to conclude that general mental ability plays more important role in giftedness. Specific abilities have their own significance. One may be gifted in a certain area but in that also 'g' factor plays the most important role, *i.e.,* without outstanding general mental ability it is not possible to be gifted in any specific area.

The intelligence tests are not free from shortcomings as one test does not include all the factors of intelligence. Therefore, some of the professionals are of the view that people who contribute significantly to the society are in real sense gifted. The statement made by ERIC Clearinghouse on Disabilities and Gifted Education is like this:

> "Giftedness is that precious endowment of potentially outstanding abilities which allows a person to interact with the environment with remarkably high levels of achievement and creativity."

One of the most widely used and popular definitions has been given by the U.S. Commissioner of Education. It is also called the Marland Report to the Congress of the United States (1972). The definition is given below:

> "Gifted and talented children are those identified by professionally qualified persons who, by virtue of outstanding abilities, are capable of high performance. These are children who require differentiated educational programmes and/or services beyond those normally provided by the regular programme in order to realize their contribution to self and society."

The report further says:

> "Children capable of high performance include those with demonstrated achievement and/or potential ability in any of the following areas, singly or in combination:
>
> - General intellectual ability
> - Specific academic aptitude
> - Creative or productive thinking
> - Leadership ability
> - Visual or performing arts
> - Psychomotor ability"

This report is quite comprehensive in nature and serves the purpose of focussing on potential and delineating a variety of ability areas. It includes high scores on mental abilities, *i.e.,* memory, vocabulary, word fluency, reasoning, numerical ability etc. The definition also says that gifted children have specific extraordinary ability in a field like literature, music, dance, science, mathematics and so on. These children have novel and original ideas and concepts. Certain qualities such as cooperation, self-confidence, high self-esteem, high level of aspiration, feeling of responsibility etc. help them to lead in any sphere of life. Although physical, spatial, mechanical and practical abilities have been included in the report in the form of psychomotor ability, but all these abilities are not considered quite significant for giftedness.

With the passage of the Gifted and Talented Children's Act of 1978 (PL 95 – 561), some modifications were made in the definition. The modified definition reads as follows:

> "Gifted and talented children means children and whenever

> applicable, youth, who are identified at the preschool, elementary or secondary level as possessing demonstrated or potential abilities that give evidence of high performance capability in areas such as intellectual, creative, specific academic, or leadership ability, or in the performing and visual arts, and who by reason thereof require services or activities not ordinarily provided by the school."

This modified form of the definition has some significant elements. Kitano and Kirby (1986) have highlighted them like this:

First, it maintains the notion that giftedness is a multidimensional concept composed of students with a wide variety of superior skills. Second, it acknowledges a wide range, from preschool through high school. Third, it includes students who demonstrate potential for superiority, not just students who have already demonstrated their superiority. Finally this definition notes that gifted and talented students need special education to meet their individual needs.

The Education Consolidation and Improvement Act of 1981 has also defined the term, though the fundamental components are the same. It says that gifted and talented students are those who give evidence of high performance capability in areas such as intellectual, creative, artistic, leadership capability, or specific academic fields, and who require services or activities not ordinarily provided by the school in order to fully develop such capabilities.

Needless to mention that all these definitions are comprehensive but to some extent they are subjective also in the sense that criteria of outstanding abilities or high performance capability are not clear. In this regard Taylor (1968) has remarked that all are gifted and talented in some way or the other. These definitions do not take gifted and talented separately rather both have the same characteristics. The fact is that gifted children have overall superior abilities while talented children have superiority in any specific area, *i.e.,* they are expert in any one or more than one areas. The speciality of talented is that he/she might excel in a specific field like music, performing art, visual art and so on.

With the passage of time the changes in the definitions of giftedness are easily seen. It was thought that only IQ cannot be the sole base of giftedness rather other factors are also included in it. Renzulli presented a definition which became very popular and recognisable throughout the 1980s. Renzulli (1986) said that gifted behaviour reflects an interaction among three basic clusters of human traits:

- *Above-average general and/or specific abilities*: By above-average ability, Renzulli means above average aptitude in any field or achievement in any area. This is different from simple above average intelligence.
- *High level of creativity*: Renzulli explains creativity as originality, *i.e.,* novelty, newness or uniqueness of ideas, concepts or theories etc. He does not agree with the divergent thinking aspect of human intellect proposed by J.P. Guilford.
- *High level of task commitment (motivation)*: It is the energy that is brought to bear on a particular problem or a specific performance area rather than a generalised trait.

This definition demands that a gifted child should have all the three components.

Renzulli opines that gifted and talented children are those who possess or are capable of developing this composite of traits and applying them to any potentially valuable area of human performance.

Sternberg and Wagner (1982) define giftedness as a kind of mental self-management. The mental management of one's life is a constructive, purposeful way that has three basic elements:

- Adapting to environment
- Selecting new environments and
- Shaping environments

These two researchers remark that the key psychological basis of intellectual giftedness resides in insight skills that include three main processes:

- Separating relevant from irrelevant information.
- Combining isolated pieces of information into a unified whole, and
- Relating newly acquired information to information acquired in the past.

Problem-solving abilities have been emphasised by these two researchers and they have viewed the gifted student as one who processes information rapidly and uses insight abilities.

Clark (1988) divides the characteristics of gifted children into five major categories:

- Cognitive (thinking)
- Affective (feeling)
- Physical
- Intuitive
- Societal

Van Tassel – Baska (1998) has explained how the notion genius has been extended to embrace creativity (Guilford, 1950; Torance, 1967), talent development (Feldhusen, 1995; Renzulli, 1994; Van Tassel – Baska, 1998), componential intelligence (Sternberg, 1986, 1991) and multiple intelligence (Gardner, 1983, 1993). Gagne (1985, 1995) remarked that giftedness should be considered as the translation of natural abilities (aptitude domain), with the help of interpersonal and environmental catalyst; into high performance talent areas. He includes in his theory a set of aptitudes or gifts which the child develops into talents through interaction with a range of internal and external catalysts. More expansion can be seen in the definition of giftedness by Gardner (1983) who proposed a theory of multiple intelligences.

Gardner and Hatch (1989) remark that these multiple intelligences are highly independent and that nearly all children and adults show distinctive profiles of strengths and weaknesses in the different kinds of intelligences. Further, they observed that all these intelligences cannot be measured through the usual types of testing but must be assessed in the natural context in which they can be exhibited. Therefore, they alongwith some other investigators have been preparing curriculum activities which allow children to develop and demonstrate all their intelligences in common or typical contexts. They cite the example that young children's intelligences may be assessed by using the kinds of materials and activities with which they have become familiar in their preschool. The definition of giftedness adopted by the 1993 Queensland Education Department Policy is as follows:

Gifted children are those who excel, or have the potential to excel, in any general or specific ability area. These criteria are outlined in the Resource Document: The education of gifted children in Queensland State Schools, 1993, should be considered alongwith other definitions available in literature. The field of gifted education relates predominantly to formal schooling and entertains two major questions. These are:

- Which students are gifted (*i.e.,* The Education of Gifted Students).
- What are their needs in terms of school organisation, curriculum content and Pedagogy (*i.e.*, Gifted Education).

Tennenbaum (2003) has proposed the definition of giftedness in a somewhat different fashion which is like this:

> "Keeping in mind that developed talent exists primarily in adults, I propose a definition of giftedness in children to denote their potential for becoming critically acclaimed performers or exemplar producers of ideas in spheres of activity that enhance the moral, physical, emotional, social, intellectual or aesthetic life of humanity."

Tennenbaum while detailing the definition says that it is useful to answer three basic questions about giftedness in its maturity, most often in adulthood:

Who qualifies to join the pool of possibly gifted individuals?

What broad realms of achievement among pool members are judged for signs of excellence?

How do pool members demonstrate their giftedness in these domains of human accomplishment?

Types

Gross's (2000) categories of giftedness can be used to describe the Intelligence Quotient assessment that form one part of the picture of a child's giftedness. She believes that intellectually gifted children can be classified as mildly, moderately, highly, exceptionally and profoundly gifted. Levels of intellectual giftedness, as defined by IQ ranges, and the level of prevalence of such children in the general population, appear as follows:

- Mildly (or basically) gifted 115 – 129 (1:6-1:40)
- Moderately gifted 130-144 (1:40 – 1:1000)
- Highly gifted 145-159 (1:1000 – 1:10,000)
- Exceptionally gifted 160-179 (1:10,000-1:1 million)
- Profoundly gifted 180 + (Fewer than 1:1 million)

Tennenbaum (2003) is of the view that there are two types of gifted people.

- Producers
- Performers

What do producers produce? Thoughts and tangibles. Further he says what do performers do? Staged artistry and human services. How do producers of thoughts, tangibles, performers of staged artistry and human services go about their excellence? By working creatively or proficiently. Tennenbaum notices that accordingly, there are eight categories of people who are recognized by Western Societies for the quality of their work. These types are given below:

1. The Producer of Thoughts, Creatively

People who are poets, novelists, dramatists or essayists, acclaimed painters, choreographers or composers belong to this category. They are the people who have their own philosophy, they do not profess others' philosophies. They are not only the lovers of the arts, not the science enthusiasts and history buffs, rather they are the theoretical or experimental scientists and real historians.

2. The Producer of Thoughts, Proficiently

People of this group are those who are masters of computers; can deal with software programmes; can solve complicated problems in the field of maths or science; have deep insight and the talent to edit the chaotic manuscript into fine literature. These people are great trouble-shooters with superior critical skills.

3. The Producer of Tangibles, Creatively

These are the people who have very high level imagination power, hence they are the inventors in science and technology and give the society new products like air conditioner, refrigerator, medical equipments, highly sophisticated communication devices etc. They are artists, sculptors, painters who use their aesthetic sense.

4. The Producer of Tangible, Proficiently

They are the master forgers of great art; diamond polishers whose perfect facets reflect light brilliantly; stone cutters who chisel intricate figures and ornaments for a cathedral's exterior; woodcrafts persons who reproduce traditional furniture faithfully in all its complicated design. They are machinists capable of constructing sophisticated and problem free equipments and machines and tool makers who work by hand to reproduce precision instruments.

5. The Performer of Staged Artistry, Creatively

Tennenbaum says that this is the interpreter or recreator. Included are the musical recitalists presenting their own understanding of composer's works; dramatic actors breathing life into a character in a play; dancers communicating their idiosyncratic rendition of a choreographed piece; poetry readers, and orchestral conductors whose brilliance lies in their unique renditions of others' works. Oratory and debate can also be fitted into this category, although some may count them among the lost arts.

6. The Performer of Staged Artistry, Proficiently

Included are dancers who translate the choreographer's art into motion faithfully, not interpretively; orchestral musicians whose technique and self discipline enable the conductor to recreate the wishes of the composer; movie actors who carry out the will of the director and thus turn movie drama into a director's art, and chorus members whose precise musical and dance performances blend easily with that of other members.

7. The Performer of Human Services, Creatively

Included are innovative teachers, political leaders, social workers, clinical psychologists, and other members of the helping professions. Also deserving mention are action researchers in medicine, the behavioural and social sciences, education and any other field that can help the human-to-human conditions.

8. The Performer of Human Services, Proficiently

These are the classroom teachers who follow guidelines faithfully and successfully; physicians with a keen mind for diagnosis and treatment; psychiatrists who are sensitive to the needs of the patients; and administrators of large corporations and service institutions who demonstrate superior managerial skills that require following a redesigned administrative plan competently, rather than designing and executing an original plan.

Renzulli and Reis have suggested that there are two types of giftedness:

Schoolhouse Giftedness

This type of giftedness is related to the school achievement of the child. This includes also the gifted who score high in various kinds of entrance examinations. It justifies the correlation between IQ and school performance of the students. The researchers have observed that this giftedness exists in various degrees; it can be identified through standardised assessment techniques ... we should, therefore, do everything in our power to make appropriate modifications for students who ... to cover regular curricular material at advanced rates and levels of understanding.

Creative Productive Giftedness

This type of giftedness is entirely different from the giftedness of school learning and achievement. For labelling a child gifted, it is essential to include this aspect in the assessment test, as it plays the most prominent role in one's life. It is the giftedness which emphasises on creativity as well as productivity potential of the child. The advocates of this type do not give much weightage to IQ score. In fact, this aspect is more advantageous for the development and progress of any society. Majority is of consumers but few are there who produce novel ideas, concepts, principles, theories or laws in different fields. The need is of the later type of people. History reveals that we remember the producers, inventors and creators not those who had high scores on IQ test as being only highly intelligent is not of much use for the society. The society needs 'really gifted' people because they help raising the standard. Renzulli (1978, 1986) considers this aspect as one of the most important rationales of Enrichment Triad Model of giftedness which is clear from his three ring conception of giftedness.

Terminology

There are some confusion regarding the terms used for giftedness. Many terms are used for it. Renzulli, Reis and Smith (1981) remark that children who have superior mental ability can confuse in this regard. *Precocity* refers to remarkable early development. Many highly gifted children show precocity in different areas of development such as language, music, mathematics, vocabulary etc. The rate of intellectual development of all gifted children exceeds the rate for non-gifted children. *Insight* may be defined as separating relevant from irrelevant information, finding novel and useful ways of combining relevant bits of information, or relating new and old information in an original and productive manners. *Genius* has sometimes been used to indicate a particular aptitude or capacity in any area. More often, it has been used to indicate extremely rare intellectual powers (extremely high IQ or creativity). *Creativity* refers to the ability to express new and useful ideas, to sense and elucidate novel and important relationship, and to ask previously unthought of, but crucial questions. The word *talent* ordinarily has been used to indicate a special ability, aptitude or accomplishment such as mechanical, musical, clerical and so on.

Myths About Gifted Children

Due to deviation in mental abilities, most of the time these children are understood in a different way. Selling and Birch (1980) have noted several myths that have been discovered about gifted and talented students. In fact, most of the myths are based on stereotypes of gifted children and each and every gifted child may have different types of strengths, weaknesses, personality traits and other characteristics. Some of the researchers (Lock and Jay, 1987) have proved sex differences on certain personality factors. They noted that gifted girls reported a more positive self-concept than did their non-gifted peers, whereas gifted boys reported a lower self-concept than did their counterparts. These children are considered as physically and emotionally weak. They are taken as socially less accepted while as a group, gifted are quite healthy in all these areas. It is thought that they are unable to adjust in school. The reality is that it is not the school, rather the whole school system is unable to satisfy and fulfil their mental needs. Hence they show undesirable behaviour and attitude toward school including teachers as well as curriculum.

Sometimes, they are considered as superhuman as they can do every type of task and solve every problem. No doubt, they have very high level of mental or cognitive abilities but they are not superhuman. Besides, people think that this group is only very highly intelligent. The fact is different. Not only intelligence, rather other cognitive factors of high level are also included in giftedness. So, if one is gifted, he/she may be highly creative also, motivated and committed to the task also. The latest definitions do not emphasise only on high IQ scores. In fact the meaning of giftedness is not still clear. Therefore, sometimes it is thought that the characteristics of giftedness are always stable. They are stable but it may also happen that in some children the giftedness is identified at an early age and thus they continue to be gifted throughout the life. But on the other hand, in some children, it is identified at a later stage. So the fact is that they were gifted but could not be recognised timely.

One most harmful misconception about these children is that since they are gifted, they do not need extra facility or help in the field of education. It is thought that since they have surplus intelligence they will perform highly in their education. Parents also have high expectations from these children without providing required educational ambience. The fact is entirely different. These children are not able to perform highly unless they are provided with the suitable curriculum, teachers, teaching methods, school ambience etc.

Some myths have been highlighted (http://www.ri.net/gifted/talented/character.html) like this:

Gifted Kids are Like Cream that Rises to the Top in a Classroom

Not necessarily. Gifted children can have hidden learning disabilities that go undiscovered because they can easily compensate for them in the early years. But as time goes on, it becomes harder and harder for them to excel. This can lead to behaviour problems and depression.

Gifted Kids are So Smart they Do Fine with or without Special Programmes

They may appear to do fine on their own. But without proper challenge they can become bored and unruly. As the years go by they may find it harder and harder as work does become more challenging, since they never faced any challenge before.

Gifted and Talented Means the Same Thing

Again not necessarily. There is no rule that states that a child who is capable of scoring to the high ninety percentiles on group achievement testing must be considered gifted. Such a child is most definitely Academically Talented. But further individualised IQ and out of level academic must be given before we can define that child as "Gifted." At the same time, there is no rule that states a child identified as gifted should be achieving so high standards in the classroom. This type of stereotyping can do serious and irreversible damage to both groups. Any child can benefit from enrichment. Academically Talented children can benefit from Honours (Grade Level) Classes. Intellectually gifted children need a differentiated curriculum and possibly even a different environment.

The Need to go Through School with Their Own Age Mates

Where it is true that children need to play and interact socially with other children their age, they do not need to learn with them. Especially in the case of a highly gifted child who may have a chronological age of six and mental age of eleven and who has been reading since two. To put that child in a reading class with other six year olds who are just learning to read is sheer torture for that child.

Giftedness is Something to be Jealous About

This is perhaps the most damaging myth. More often than not gifted children can feel isolated and misunderstood. They have more adult tastes in music, clothing, reading material and food. These differences with other children can cause them to be shunned and even abused verbally or physically by other children. Experts in the field of gifted education are beginning to address the higher incidences of ADHD and spelling/handwriting disabilities in the gifted population verses those in the much larger normal population.

Terman's Study

Lewis M. Terman (1877-1956) was impressed by Sir Francis Galton, Alfred Binet and their contemporaries. He was asked to prepare two reports, one on mental deficiency and one on genius when he was a senior at Indiana University. He graduated from a normal college and taught for five years in schools. Till that time he was not aware of mental tests. He completed his post-graduation with thesis on leadership among children. The thesis was based in part on tests used by Binet. These tests were in Binet's studies of suggestibility.

When Terman joined Clark University for his Ph.D. in education and psychology under the guidance of G. Stanley Hall, there were some myths about children with high mental abilities. He devoted much time to study and wonder about precocious children. During that time it was thought that these children had some mental diseases like psychoticism or neuroticism as they did not behave in a normal manner. During that time a slogan:

"Early ripe, early rot"

had developed which means that the child whose developments are early, it was sure that he/she would one day become totally abnormal. But the idea that how a child with early development and higher mental abilities differs from child with mental backwardness led Terman to choose the topic for his doctoral dissertation. He conducted an experimental study for which he selected fourteen male children, out of which seven were brightest and seven dullest in a large city school. Various intelligence tests constructed by Binet and some other tests were administered to all the fourteen subjects. Terman says that the results of that study could contribute to the science very little or might be nothing but the results contributed a lot to his future thinking. He joined the faculty of Stanford University in 1910. In 1922 he became the head of the psychology department and retired from the same post in 1942. Binet's tests were published in 1905 and 1908, Terman revised the 1908 test tentatively. Many more revisions were made in this test and the test was published in 1916. Terman had also developed the Army Alpha and Beta tests for use in classifying servicemen during World War I. These were the first group intelligence tests. But it is Terman who introduced the term IQ when he published the Stanford – Binet Intelligence Test in 1916. The term after that received much popularity (Irvine, 2000). Again it was revised in 1937. The test was standardised on one thousand children whose IQ range was from 60 to 145. The study fascinated Terman to the extent that after this, he decided to do work on this very population in future. In fact, it took the shape of a dream of Terman to know about these children in detail.

In 1921, Terman was sanctioned a financial grant from the Commonwealth Fund of New York City which helped him locating one thousand children with the IQ level of 140 or higher. The Stanford Binet tests helped selecting children from Kindergarten to eighth grade for the study. Apart from this, a group mental test was also administered. Thus the number of subjects to be studied rose to 1500 with average IQ of 150.

The purpose of the studies were to find out the traits of children who had high IQ. Secondly, to follow those children for a long time to know what changes took place in them when they became adults. Physical measurements, medical examinations, interest tests character tests, achievement tests, trait ratings and some other information were collected by Terman from parents and teachers. Important results were like this:

Children of IQ 140 or higher were in general, appreciably superior to unselected children in physique, health and social adjustment. They were markedly superior in moral attitudes as measured either by character tests or by trait ratings; and vastly superior in their mastery of school subjects. In fact, the typical child of the group had mastered the school subjects to a point about two grades beyond the one in which he was enrolled, and some of them three or four grades beyond.

Moreover, the child's ability as evidenced by achievement in different school subjects was so general as to refute completely the traditional belief that gifted children were usually one sided. Terman says that he felt pride in the fact that not one of the major conclusions drawn in the early 1920s regarding the traits that were typical of gifted children had been overthrown in the three decades since then.

The study revealed that incidence of mortality, ill health, insanity and alcoholism was below that for the generality of corresponding age. Further, it was also found that the subjects under study were well adjusted in society and less delinquency was also found. These subjects showed superior intelligence in their adulthood also. Thus the notion "Early ripe, early rot" was totally discarded by Terman. The subjects after completing their schooling, about 90 per cent of them joined colleges and 70 per cent joined graduation courses. 30 per cent students were awarded graduation with honours. About two third remained for graduate work. The educational achievement of those subjects could not be recorded because of the duration of Great Depression. But Terman was sure enough that they would have performed better than their general counterparts. The study reveals that during under-graduation, 40 per cent of male and 20 per cent of female students earned half or more of their college expenses. The subjects were quite cooperative in nature which is supported by the fact that the researcher was able to keep track of more than 80 per cent of the original group. Case histories of women could not be prepared as the number of women who went to the level of choosing career was very less. But the case histories of 800 men were prepared in 1950. The histories revealed that when the men had an average age of 40 years, they had published 67 books, out of which 46 were in the fields of science, arts and humanities and 21 were of fictions. 1,400 technical, scientific and professional articles had been published by them; more than 200 plays, novelettes and short stories had been published and about 236 articles on various topics or areas were written and published as well. More than 150 patents had been written by these adults. Besides, they wrote many other articles for journals, news stories, editorials, T.V. scripts, radio-scripts and newspaper columns as well.

The case histories revealed that out of the total 800 men, 78 completed the doctoral work or its equivalent, 85 received law degree, 48 medical degree, 51 had done basic research in the physical sciences and engineering, 74 taught or had taught in a four year college or university and 104 who were basically engineers but they had done only applied research or none. The remarkable point is that 47 scientists were listed in the 1949 edition of American Men of Science which was of high repute. Terman observed that nearly all of these numbers were from 10 to 20 or 30 times as large as would be found for 800 men of corresponding age picked at random in the general population and were sufficient answer to those who belittle the significance of IQ differences.

Terman says that general intelligence, *i.e.,* 'g' factor of Spearman contributes a lot in making a scientist, artist, poet, musician, mechanic etc. He opines that to achieve greatly in almost any field, the special talents have to be backed up by a lot of Spearman's 'g' by which is meant the kind of general intelligence that requires ability to form many sharply defined concepts, to manipulate them and to perceive subtle relationship between them; in other words the ability to engage in abstract thinking. Terman refers to the study conducted by Cox (1926) in the support of contribution of 'g' factor. He remarks that Cox's study was the part of his original plan to investigate superior ability by two methods of approach:

- by identifying and following living gifted subjects from childhood onwards.
- by proceeding in the opposite direction and tracing the mature genius back to his childhood promise.

Cox's study (magnum opus) was – *The Early Mental Traits of Three Hundred Geniuses*. Her subjects represented an unbiased selection from the top 510 in Cattell's objectively compiled list of 1000 most eminent men of history. 3000 biographies were scanned by Cox for getting the information that would throw light on the early development of the subjects. After a detailed study Cox concluded that "the genius who achieves highest eminence is one whose intelligence test would have identified as gifted in childhood."

Terman cites some of the examples of geniuses who had not been assessed in a desirable way. He says that one of them was Oliver Goldsmith. His childhood teacher is said to have said – "Never was so dull a boy." The fact was that little Oliver was writing clever verse at the age of seven and at eight he was reading Ovid and Horace. Another was Sir Walter Scott, who at seven not only read widely in poetry but was using correctly in his written prose such words as 'melancholy' and 'exotic'. Other alleged childhood dullards include a number who disliked the usual diet of Latin and Greek but had natural talent for science. Among these were the celebrated German Chemist Justus Von Liebig, the great English anatomist John Hunter, and the naturalist Alexander Von Humboldt, whose name is scattered so widely over the maps of the world.

Special characteristics of gifted are visible in early childhood. Terman tried to know the results of the study by Cox (1926) in this regard. It was noted that marked foreshadowing could be seen in the case of more than half of the group, none at all in less than a fourth. For example, Macaulay began his career as a historian at the age of six with what he called a "Campendium of Universal History." Ben Franklin showed the characteristics of giftedness before the age of seventeen including scientific curiosity, religious heterodoxy, wit and buffoonery, political and business shrewdness and writing ability. Pascal showed high level of interest in mathematics. The level of interest compelled his father to deprive him of the mathematics books until he had first mastered Latin and Greek. It is interesting to know that Pascal secretly proceeded to construct a geometry of his own and covered the ground as far as the thirty second proposition of Euclid. This led his father to show the mild behaviour. Another example is of Leibnitz who at the age of fourteen started to write on logic and philosophy and composing what he called "An Alphabet of Human thought."

Terman in his study observes that the case histories of his study's sample also showed the behaviour characteristics of giftedness at an early age. He compared scientists and non-scientists among the eight hundred gifted men. He found many highly significant differences between the early interests and social attitudes of those who became physical scientists and those who showed expertise in the social sciences, law or the humanities. Those in medical or biological sciences usually rated on such variables somewhere between the physical scientists and non-scientists.

Terman emphasises much on 'g' factor and says that ability tests which are able to measure general intelligence can successfully choose the gifted in childhood. Regarding Thurstone's primary mental abilities, Terman said that the factor analysts don't agree on how many "primary" mental abilities there were nor exactly on what they were. In fact the experts in the field were divided into two groups. One group belonged to British representatives like Burt, Thomson and Vernon who had the view of three or four group factors in addition to 'g'. Another group belonged to Americans who thought that there were about fifteen separate factors. British experts did not believe in minor group factors and some Americans also were of the same viewpoint. For the reality of group factors, Terman felt the need of further research.

Terman emphasised on the importance of early discovery of exceptional abilities. In support of his view he quoted monumental studies by Lehman (1953) in which he has found out the relationship between age and creative achievement. Terman says that the striking thing about age curves was how early in life the period of maximum creativity was reached. The results revealed that in nearly all fields of science, the best work is done between ages twenty five and thirty five and rarely later than forty. The studies revealed that the peak productivity for works of lesser merit was usually reached five to ten years later; this was true in some twenty fields of science, in philosophy, in most kinds of musical composition, in art and in literature of many varieties. Lehman's studies' implications were that the youth of high achievement potential should be well trained for his life work before too many of his most creative years had been passed.

Lehman's studies raised the issue of acceleration for the gifted. Terman was of the view that it seemed that the schools were more opposed to acceleration then than were thirty years ago when he had conducted his study. He says that the lockstep seemed to have become more and more the fashion, notwithstanding the fact that practically everyone who had investigated the subject was against that. It is revealed that 29 per cent of his gifted group managed to graduate from high school before the age of sixteen and half years (62 of these before fifteen and half). 71 per cent graduated between sixteen and half and eighteen and half. Comparisons were made between accelerated and non-accelerated on many factors. The two groups differed very little in childhood IQ, their health records were equally good and as adults they were found equally well adjusted in society. More of the accelerated, graduated from college and on the average nearly a year and a half earlier than the non-accelerates. They averaged higher in college grades and more often remained for graduate work. It was also found that the accelerates on the average married .7 of a year earlier, had a trifle lower divorce rate and scored just a little higher when their marital happiness was measured (Terman and Oden, 1947). The results regarding the college records of accelerates and non-accelerates were similar to those of the study conducted by Keys (1938) and Pressey (1949).

Terman refers to the Ford Fund for the Advancement of Education (1953) which awarded annually since 1951 some four hundred college scholarships to gifted students who were not over sixteen and half years old, were a year or even two years short of high school graduation but showed good evidence of ability to do college work. Three quarters of them were between fifteen and half and sixteen and half at the time of college entrance. About twelve colleges and universities accepted those students and were keeping close track of their success. A summary of their records for the first year showed that they not only got higher grades than their classmates, who averaged about two years older but they were also equally socially well adjusted and participated in as many extra-curricular activities. It is also stated that the main problem the boys had was in finding girls to date who were not too old for them. Some of them had started a campaign to remedy the situation by urging that more of those scholarships be awarded to girls. Terman is of the view that children with 140 IQ should be promoted rapidly enough to permit college entrance by the age seventeen at least, and that a majority would be better off to enter at sixteen. The exceptionally bright student who is kept with his age group finds little to challenge his intelligence and all too often develops habits of laziness that later wreck his college career. He gives the example of the case of a college student who was preparing for a profession in science, medicine, law or any field of advanced scholarship, graduation at twenty instead of the usual twenty two means two years added to his professional career or the two years saved could be used for additional training beyond the doctorate if that were deemed preferable.

Terman cites the study conducted by Learned and Wood (1938)

who had shown by objective achievement tests in some forty Pennsylvania Colleges how little correlation there was between the student's knowledge and the number of months or years of his college attendance. They found some beginning sophomores who had acquired more knowledge than some seniors near their graduation. Both the researchers found similarly low correlations between the number of course units a student had in a given field and the amount he knew in that field. Some with only one year of Latin had learned more than others with three years. They even found boys just graduating from high school who had more knowledge of science than some college seniors who had majored in science and were about to begin teaching science in high schools.

Regarding measuring instruments, Terman says that instruments that helped the identifications of gifted students were available in great variety and at nearly all levels from primary grades to the graduate schools or universities. He said that tests of achievement in the school subjects at that time were being given in his country to children below high school at a rate of perhaps ten or twelve million a year and to high school students another million or two. In addition, perhaps two million tests of intelligence were given annually in the elementary and high schools. During the studies conducted by Terman the movement of testing spread rapidly in many countries including Britain and the Commonwealth countries. A test was developed by Thomson (1921) which later was called the Moray House Test of Intelligence. This test helped selecting the more gifted eleven year old children in the primary schools for the privilege of free secondary education. After revision, the test was administered annually on about a half million scholarship candidates. This test had included history, mathematics and English tests. The Scottish Council for Research in Education (1933) administered the Moray House test of intelligence which was a group test on all the ninety thousand children in Scotland born in 1921. Though the test was administered on a larger sample but actually it tested only eighty seven thousand of the total population, *i.e.,* ninety thousand children. The Stanford Binet tests had been translated and adapted in almost all the European, Asian countries and Latin America also for measuring intelligence. Terman revealed the fact and said that behind the iron curtain, there was a ban on mental tests.

During the studies by Terman different personality tests became popular which included personality inventories, attitude scales, projective techniques, interest tests, leadership tests, tests of pscyhoticism and pre-delinquent tendencies, tests of masculinity and femininity and marital aptitude tests and so on. Thereafter, Terman speaks about education of gifted children also. Acceleration of a year or two or three however, desirable, was but a fraction of what was needed to keep the gifted child or youth working at his intellectual best. The method most often advocated was curriculum enrichment for the gifted without segregating them from the ordinary class. Under ideal conditions enrichment could accomplish much, but since schools were overcrowded, teachers were overworked, underpaid and not trained properly, curriculum enrichment for a few gifted in a large mixed class could not begin to solve the problem.

Terman and Oden (1947) made an attempt to identify some of the non-intellectual factors that influenced the life success among the men in their gifted group. Three judges, working independently, examined the records of the seven hundred and thirty men who were then twenty five years old or older and rated each on life success. The criterion of "success" was the extent to which a subject had made use of his superior intellectual ability, little weight was given to earned income. The one hundred and fifty men rated highest for success and the one hundred and fifty rated lowest were then compared on some two hundred items of information obtained from childhood onward. The difference between the two groups was as follows:

The two groups were called As and Cs. Both the groups were almost equally successful during the elementary school years. The average grades were about the same, and average scores on achievement tests were only a little higher for the As. Early in high school, the groups began to draw apart in scholarship, and by the end of high school the slump of the Cs was quite marked. The slump could not be blamed on extra-curricular activities, for those were almost twice as common among the As. Nor was much of it due to difference in intelligence. Although the As tested on the average a little higher than the Cs both in 1922 and 1940, the average score made by the Cs in 1940 was high enough to permit brilliant college work, in fact was equalled by only 15 per cent of highly selected Stanford students. Of the As, 97 per cent entered college and 90 per cent graduated; of the

Cs 68 per cent entered but only 37 per cent graduated. Of those who graduated, 52 per cent of the As but only 14 per cent of the Cs graduated with honours. The As were also more accelerated in school; on the average they were six months younger on completing the eight grade, ten months younger at high school graduation and fifteen months younger at graduation from colleges.

The difference between the educational histories of the As and Cs reflect to some degree the differences in their family background. Half of the A fathers but only fifteen percent of the C fathers were college graduates, and twice as many of A siblings as of C siblings graduated. The estimated number of books in the A homes was nearly 50 per cent greater than in the C homes. As of 1928, when the average age of the subjects was about sixteen years, more than twice as many of the C parents as of A parents had been divorced.

Terman and Oden further found interesting differences between the groups. Both the groups differed in the childhood data on emotional stability, social adjustment and various traits of personality. Of the twenty five traits on which each child was rated by parent and teacher in 1922 (eighteen years before the A and C groups were made up), the only trait on which the Cs averaged as high as the As was general health. The superiority of the As was especially marked in four volitional traits: prudence, self confidence, perseverance and desire to excel. The As also rated significantly higher in 1922 on leadership, popularity and sensitiveness to approval or disapproval. By 1940 the difference between the groups in social adjustment and all round mental stability had greatly increased and showed itself in many ways. By that time four-fifths of the As had married, but only two-thirds of the Cs and the divorce rate for those who had married was twice as high for the Cs as for the As. Moreover, the As made better marriages; their wives on the average came from better homes, were better educated and scored higher on intelligence tests.

The researchers further remark that the most spectacular differences between the two groups came from three sets of ratings, made in 1940, on about twelve personality traits. Each man rated himself on all the traits, was rated on them by his wife if he had a wife and by a parent if a parent was still living. Although the three sets of ratings were made independently, they agreed unanimously on the four traits in which the A and C groups differed most widely. They were "persistence in the accomplishment of ends," "integration toward goals, as contrasted with drifting," "self-confidence", and "freedom from inferiority feelings". For each trait three critical ratios were computed showing, respectively, the reliability of the A-C difference in average of self-ratings, ratings by wives, and ratings by parents. The average of the three critical ratios was 5.5 for perseverance, 5.6 for integration toward goals, 3.7 for self confidence, and 3.1 for freedom from inferiority feelings. These were similar to the traits that Cox (1926) found in one hundred leading geniuses whom she rated on many aspects of personality; their three outstanding traits she defined as "persistence of motive and effort", "confidence in their abilities," and "strength or force of character."

Terman says that there was one trait on which only the parents of their A and C men were asked to rate them; that trait was designated "common sense." As judged by parents, the As were again reliably superior, the A-C difference in average rating had a critical ratio of 3.9. Everything considered, there was nothing in which A and C groups presented a greater contrast than in drive to achieve and in all-around mental and social adjustment. Terman and Oden's (1947) data did not corroborate the findings by Lange-Eichbaum (1932) in which it was concluded that great achievement usually stems from emotional tensions that border on the abnormal. In Terman's gifted group, success was related with stability rather than instability, with absence rather than with presence of disturbing conflicts – in short with well-balanced temperament and with freedom from excessive frustrations.

To summarise it can be said that Terman's subjects were in a 1500-child sample (800 males and 700 females) that was in the top one percent of the school population in measured intelligence; *i.e.* they possessed tested IQs of 140 or higher (Terman and Oden, 1925). Terman and Oden (1951) summarised the characteristics of the students in the sample as:

- slightly larger, healthier and more physically attractive
- superior in reading, language usage, arithmetical reasoning, science, literature and the arts
- superior in arithmetical computation, spelling and factual information about history and civics
- spontaneous, with variety of interests, able to learn to read

easily and able to read more and better books than average children
- less inclined to boast or overstate their knowledge
- more emotionally stable, different in the upward direction for nearly all traits.

Follow up studies in 1947, 1951 and 1959 were completed to obtain a comparison between promise and performance (Bauer, 2000). Feldman (1984) opines that follow up studies by other investigators have obtained less "perfect" findings, in that not all of the subjects were found to be geniuses in the sense of transcendent achievement in some fields. However, recent studies corroborate the study by Terman on some traits like spontaneity and creativity in play (Barnett and Fiscella, 1985), emotional stability (Schlowinski and Reynolds, 1985) and reading aptitude (Anderson, Tollefson and Gillbert, 1985). This makes clear that follow up studies are still being conducted. Bauer (2000) opines that the entire set of data sources for Terman's original group is maintained in closed files at Stanford University. It is estimated that less than half of the closed responses of this source of data have been transferred to tabulation sheets.

No doubt that Terman has the credit of starting the movement of gifted. He contributed in the form of special educational adaptation for gifted children so that their potentials can be harnessed in a desirable fashion.

Criticism of Terman's Study

Terman's is a monumental study in the field of gifted children including their identification, characteristics and education. Needless to mention that not even a single research work is perfect and complete in itself. Researchers have reviewed his study thoroughly and raised some objections on certain significant issues such as:

- Criteria of identifying gifted children
- Characteristics of gifted children and
- Education of these children

Like a true researcher, Terman also had accepted that there might be some shortcomings in his longitudinal study which helped him including his name in the list of one of the great psychologists. He has stated in the summary chapter of his classic Genetic Studies of Genius:

> "If the methods that have been employed have at times led to erroneous conclusions, these in time will be discovered and corrected. One who suspects error at any point has only to apply the same or demonstrably better objective methods to test the justness of his suspicions. It is to be hoped that sooner or later all our conclusions will thus be put to trial.
>
> The ultimate value of our study will be measured more by the investigations which it stimulates or provokes others ... by the amount of its factual data that later experiments may verify" (Terman, 1925)

The re-evaluation of Terman's study should be taken in a positive way and with healthy attitude which gives the proper guidance to future researchers. Many investigators have expressed their views on the methodology adopted by Terman. Surprisingly very few have raised their objections on the characteristics of gifted children. Hughes and Converse (1965) showed their concern with the contrast between the number with IQs of 140 or above (approximately 0.4%) located in Terman's search for the gifted and the number with IQs of 140 or more (1.1%) in the 1937 revision of the Standford-Binet. The main experimental group of 643 (not 1000 as seems to be commonly believed) in Terman's study was obtained from a canvass of a school population of 159,812 students. Another group, drawn from a second population not clearly specified in his report, composed the remainder of the group typically known as the 1000 gifted children. This second group was tested by volunteers and drawn from cities both in California and outside the state. Based upon the percentage (1.1%) of the 1937 standardisation group of the Stanford-Binet with IQs above 140, Terman should have located approximately 1758 cases with IQs above 140 from the 159,812. (More should have been located if the second population, from which the remaining members of the 1000 gifted were drawn, is included but information on this group is too inadequate to permit any projections). By lowering cut-off point to 135 there should have been an additional 1600 cases for a total of 3358 from the 159,812. According to Hughes and Converse this is over five times the 643 Terman actually located.

Sample Selection

Hughes and Converse (1956) highlight the weaknesses in selecting the sample. On the basis of evidence in literature on low and under achievement they suggested that an interaction between selection methods and personality factors in achievement caused proportionately too few children to be identified as gifted in many of the populations under study. Fliegler and Bish (1959) summarising 251 studies in a review were concerned about the narrow definition of giftedness (typically by tests of intelligence). However, they did not give sufficient evidence of concern over the sampling methods and procedures generally used for selection of gifted children. They suggested:

> "The conglomerate characteristics extensively illustrated and described by Terman and Oden need still further definition and clarification if the potentially gifted are to be described."

In a study reported by Lewis (1940) in which he questioned Terman's method of selection, approximately 50,000 children were canvassed in grades four to eight. The teachers were asked to rate any child as extremely mentally retarded, genius, or as a distinct problem; they selected 341 children as geniuses. Of this group, only 57 per cent fell within the top 10 per cent in mental ability on the Kuhlmann-Anderson Test. Barbe (1965) found evidence of a skewed distribution in a sample of 456 gifted due to a disproportionate representation of certain racial groups. Barbe observed that his method of selection and sampling techniques could well have resulted in the selection of a sample which had too many subjects in the 160 – and – above intelligence score range. It will not be out of place to mention here that Terman (1925) listed as one of his problems the fact that his group contained an unexpectedly large proportion of cases in the upper intelligence score ranges.

The analysis of Terman's study reveals that the data on group II were not summarised due to inadequate information, yet some of this group are included in the group more popularly known as the 1000 gifted children (Barbe 1965). Besides, the field assistants had the freedom to adopt the method of sample selection because of their convenience and also to save the time. Terman (1925) justifies this like:

> "... make the search more effective."

In a study, Pegnato and Birch (1959) selected approximately 1400 children from grades seven through nine. They compared the efficiency and effectiveness of seven different means of locating gifted subjects using the test criterion of a Stanford-Binet IQ of 136 or higher. Significantly the teachers missed by ratings more than half of the gifted as measured by the intelligence test score of 136 on the Stanford-Binet while 31.4 per cent of those named by them as gifted were of average intelligence on the Stanford-Binet. Levinson (1956) found inconsistencies in identification procedures which tend to favour children from the middle socio-economic level. It was proposed that separate norms for different socio-economic levels be established at the 98th percentile.

Barbe (1965) has pointed out that in the entire study the cut off points are different like 130, 135 or 140. Yet in the main experimental group of 643 pupils, 21 cases were included whose correlated IQs were in the interval 135-139 and one in the interval 130-134. These cases were included because of indications that the Binet score, due to conditions of examination was lower than it should have been. Terman (1925) himself accepts the bias in sample selection by stating that several cases were included because they were siblings of children who had already qualified; a few were included because of special interest of an investigator in a particular child.

Use of Tests of Intelligence

The reliability and validity of group intelligence tests is doubtful. This is corroborated by the analysis of the National Intelligence Tests (National B). Apart from this, Terman used norms established on the school population in California, while he discounted the original norms for this test. Regardless of the basis of his logic, in the light of his later generalisations this arbitrary decision does not seem justified (Barbe, 1956). Highsmith (1925) also criticised Terman's study and made a comprehensive study of the test and concluded that the rate of response to material in a test such as the National B is by no means an adequate measure of intelligence. Poor readers, slow starters, and test – anxious children could be several handicapped on such a test. On the one hand, Terman did not feel that such children would be missed, but on the other hand, he was concerned that the slightly less accelerated, excessively shy, or lazy child might be overlooked by his selection method. Ballard (1922) directly criticised the reliability of the National B on the basis that it has to be worked at break-neck speed; it picks out the rapid thinkers, and it leaves the profound thinkers. So it is quite clear that the measuring instrument used for the selection of the gifted group has played its role in selecting not really gifted children.

Characteristics

Terman's sample was selected following two steps:

First, they were rated by their teachers and secondly, they were evaluated on the basis of group test of intelligence. After crossing these two steps the sample had to perform an individual intelligence tests. There were fair chances that a disproportionately large number of scholastically and emotionally maladjusted cases could have been missed and thus led Terman to draw a very positive picture about the characteristics of these children.

In view of all these limitations, it is quite obvious that new researches in the field are needed. Barbe (1965) has suggested a general outline for such an investigation:

1. Define a representative sample of school children at each grade level considering the variables of sex, race, socio-economic level, geographical location, size of school enrolment, and type of school (public, parochial, or private).
2. Screen the sample of gifted children by replicating Terman's method of selection.
3. Screen the sample of gifted children by testing all the children in the sample with an individual test of intelligence; this is

the only alternative guaranteeing an accurate evaluation of the number of high scores in the sample and thus permitting a rigorous comparison with Terman's method.

4. Identify control group whose test scores fall below the score used as the criterion for giftedness.
5. In addition, obtain scores from all children in the sample on measures of creativity, curiosity, and achievement using standard procedures and identical measures throughout.
6. Identify high scores and appropriate control groups on each of the measures.
7. Analyse the degree of overlap among the methods and measures.
8. Compare the characteristics of the different groups chosen, and prepare a composite description of each group.

The above discussion reveals that some lacunae are there in Terman's study which might have presented a different picture of gifted children. But still the authoress notices that no such study has been conducted so far which is so exhaustive, informative and detailed in nature. Doubtlessly Terman has done a remarkable work in the field that is why he is considered as one of the great psychologists.

3

Characteristics of the Gifted

While discussing the characteristics of gifted children, most of the time a wrong notion among people is found that there do not exist individual differences among these children. The fact is that a gifted child may differ from another one. Not only individual differences but intra-individual differences are also found among gifted children. Telford and Sawrey (1977) opine that to assume homogeneity among the gifted would be to ignore the fact that the restriction of any one variable does not have an equally restrictive effect on other variables, even though they may be highly correlated. They cite the example that if a group of people, all of whom are six feet or over in height, is selected for investigation, it will also entail some selection on the basis of weight. Tall people tend to weigh more than short ones. But the restriction of the variability of weight will not be as great as the restriction imposed on height, even though the two are positively correlated.

Generally it was thought before Terman's study that gifted are not always fit into the society. But after Terman studied this population scientifically, the truth came before us regarding the characteristics of this group. Superior cognitive abilities affect the total behaviour of the child that includes a number of aspects of one's personality. It is not possible to do justice with this population unless their special features or characteristics are studied. Researchers have been trying to study these children from time to time, keeping in view different personal as well as non-personal aspects.

Personal and Social

The review of literature related to characteristics of gifted population reveals that very few attempts have been made to study the development of this population in detail except Terman's study. Perhaps this is the reason that many myths about this population have developed in the minds of general society.

In the beginning gifted were considered as emotionally disturbed leading to maladjustment. Lombroso (1905) spread the thinking that genius was a result of psychosis and degeneracy. This view was corroborated by Lange-Eichbaum in 1932 who said that psychosis was characteristic of many geniuses and that even when actual psychosis was not identified, many psychopathic traits could be found in a great majority of eminent personalities. But these views were proved wrong by Cox (1926), Terman (1925) and Ellis (1926). But despite these researchers' findings the myths remained among the society. It was thought that since gifted show precocity in all the areas, they become emotionally and socially misfit in the society. They were considered less sociable who even do not know how to behave with others. Some of the researches in the field of gifted children reveal a general consensus on the point that gifted if considered as a group have positive and favourable personality as well as social characteristics. Among them Terman's work is most authentic. Terman *et al.* (1925) researched the personal and social characteristics of a group of five hundred gifted children and a like number of children in an unselected control group. The results of the research revealed that gifted intellectual superiority is positively related to personal and social characteristics refuting the notion that this population is most of the time found maladjusted. It was reported that from 60 to 80 per cent of the gifted exceeded the median scores on the separate tests of the battery employed. The study also showed that these children were significantly freer from psychopathic trends and significantly more emotionally stable than were control group. Burks, Jensen and Terman (1930) and Oden (1968) favoured the view that the superiority in emotional stability was maintained for a number of years when they were examined again.

Terman on the basis of his study reached the result that gifted were not eccentric. He remarked that "eccentricity of genius is a myth." But Witty and Lehman (1929a) were not ready to accept this conclusion and showed their reluctance on this point. They observed that the assumption that the eccentricity of genius is largely a myth is probably an example of hasty generalisation. They again attacked Terman's results and remarked that it was not necessary that every recognised genius was a gifted child. They said that it was perhaps unfortunate that Terman chose to call his research Genetic Studies of Genius in the sense that his study was of children found to be intellectually superior. There was no justification in assuming that merely because his subjects were intellectually superior, they would become geniuses. Witty and Lehman (1929b) wrote an article *Nervous instability and genius* and opined that the term nervous instability, like the term genius is difficult to describe and delimit. On the other hand Hollingworth (1926) has her own ideas about the term genius. She is of the view that the term genius should be reserved to describe individuals who have already made original contributions of outstanding and lasting worth.

Many professionals of the field are of the view that superior personality and character traits are found in gifted children. Terman concluded that these children have character traits and superior personality. They are more trustworthy when under temptation to cheat, less inclined than average children to boast or to overstate their knowledge. They have more wholesome reading preferences, character preferences and social attitudes and score higher in emotional stability. Hollingworth (1926) analysed gifted children and found that children selected wholly by intelligence tests without consideration of other factors, show desirable traits of character and temperament in superior degree. They were also found more cooperative, and may be disciplined more readily than ordinary children by appeals to reason, hero worship, presenting another point of view, and consistently rewarding merit. She also found them above average in nervous stability and few among them were neurotics. They were greatly interested in play and tended strongly to choose playmates of their own mental age resulting often in social grouping with older children. They showed characteristics of reading preferences. Moreover, Hollingworth's study reveals that they were more interested in dictionaries, encyclopaedias and atlases before they were ten years old than most people ever are.

Terman and Oden (1947) arrived on conclusions on gifted children's composite portrait. They remarked that one can find within the group individual examples of almost every type of personality defect, social maladjustment, behaviour problems, and physical fraility;

the only difference is that among gifted children the incidence of these deviations is, in varying degrees, lower than in the general population. The investigators also remarked that there is no certainty that the relationship between intelligence and character present during childhood persists throughout the life, although a majority of psychologists believes that it does. Terman administered the Wyman Interest Test on gifted children. He found that ninety per cent of the gifted scored above the average of unselected children in intellectual interests and eighty-four per cent scored above the average in social interest but in activity interest, the gifted differed little from the average. It was also found that the gifted acquire far more knowledge of plays and games than the average child of their age. Their preferences among plays, games and amusements follow the normal sex trends fairly closely, but gifted girls tend to be more masculine in play interest than average girls. The play preferences of the gifted were found two or three years beyond their age norms in interest maturity. Terman's study also revealed that nearly half of the children learned to read before going to school. They learned to read easily, read more and better books than the average child, and largely educated themselves. They read over a considerably wider range than average children. They particularly read more science, history, biography, travel books, folk tales, informational fiction, poetry and drama and proportionately fewer books of adventures or mystery and far less emotional fiction. It was also reported that the vast majority of gifted children like school. They are more interested than unselected children in the more abstract subjects and somewhat less interested in the more practical subjects. The scholastic interests of gifted girls resemble those of gifted boys much more than they resemble those of average girls.

Roe (1953) attempted to investigate the social and personality characteristics of living gifted persons. Projective assessment and clinical interviews were employed to collect the data. It was found that although these people were characterised by somewhat unusual personalities and patterns of daily living, they could hardly be called maladjusted. Many other researchers such as McClelland (1962), MacKinnon (1962), Cattell (1970) and Gough (1961) corroborate Roe's findings. Refuting the misconception about the personal, social as well as emotional adjustment of gifted population, it has been confirmed that in all the fields of life this group is very well adjusted.

It has been proved by Wilson (1957), Ramaseshan (1957), Boehm (1962), Parkyn (1948), McGinn (1976), Gallagher (1975), Ketcham and Synder (1977), Keating (1974), Milgram and Milgram (1976), Lightfoot (1951), Hitch field (1973) and Mensch (1950). Sears (1977) survey has revealed that satisfaction in family life and stability of marriage were best predicted by social adjustment in childhood, good mental health as a young adult, retrospective positive attitude towards parents (measured at age forty) and a test of marital happiness given at age thirty.

Clark (1979), however, has described the characteristics of affective domain of gifted children. They are as follows:

(*a*) *Large accumulation of information about emotions that has not been brought to awareness*: The child having this characteristic needs to process cognitively the emotional meaning of experience, to name one's own emotions, to identify one's own and other's perceptual filters and defence systems, to expand and clarify awareness of the physical environment, to clarify awareness of the needs and feelings of others. The problem before the child may come in the shape of information misinterpreted affecting him/her negatively.

(*b*) *Unusual sensitivity to the expectations and feelings of others*: Needs related to this characteristic are to learn to clarify the feelings and expectations of others. The child may have to face some problems like unusual vulnerability to criticism of others, high level of need for success and recognition.

(*c*) *Keen sense of humour may be gentle or hostile*: With this characteristic, the gifted needs to learn how behaviour affects the feelings and behaviour of others. On the other hand chances of problems are also there such as use of humour for critical attack upon others resulting in damage to interpersonal relationships.

(*d*) *Heightened self-awareness, accompanied by feelings of being different*: Child with this special feature needs to learn to assert own needs and feelings non-defensively, to share self with others, for self-clarification. But the gifted child may develop isolated self, resulting in being considered aloof, feeling rejected, perceive difference as a negative attribute resulting in low self-esteem and inhibited growth emotionally and socially.

(*e*) *Idealism and sense of justice which appear at an early age*: Efforts should be made to enable the child to transcend negative reactions by finding values to which *he* or *she* can be committed. Chances are there that the gifted child may attempt unrealistic reforms and goals with resulting intense frustration (suicides result from intense depression over issues of this nature).

(*f*) *Earlier development of an inner focus of control and satisfaction*: Special needs of the child are to clarify personal priorities among conflicting values and to confront and interact with the value system of others. Possible concomitant problems are difficulty conforming; reject external validation and choose to live by personal values which may be seen as a challenge to authority or tradition.

(*g*) *Unusual emotional depth and intensity*: Related needs are to find purpose and direction from personal value system. Besides, to translate commitment into action in daily life is another need. But the child may face the problem of unusual vulnerability; problem focusing on realistic goals for life's work.

(*h*) *High expectations of self and others, often leading to high levels of frustration with self, others, and situations*: The special needs of the child are to learn to set realistic goals and to accept set-backs as part of the learning process. Possible problems are discouragement and frustration from high levels of self-criticism, problems maintaining good interpersonal relations as others fail to maintain high standards imposed by gifted individual; immobilization of action due to high levels of frustration resulting from situations which do not meet expectations of excellence.

(*i*) *Strong need for consistency between abstract values and personal actions*: Examples of related needs are to find a vocation that provides opportunity for actualisation of student's personal value system, as well as an avenue for his/her talents and abilities. Some problems the child may have like frustration with self and others leading to inhibited actualisation of self and interpersonal relationships.

(*j*) *Advanced levels of moral judgement*: The child's need is to receive validation for non-average morality. On the other hand he may have to face the problems of intolerance and lack of understanding from peer group, leading to rejection and possible isolation.

Strang feels the need of guidance to gifted children regarding their personal adjustment and remarks that the reasons for maintaining good mental health among gifted groups differ only in degree from the reasons for maintaining mental health in the average population. It is further remarked that in a democratic society which depends upon the continued development of intelligent leaders, the mental health of future leaders is most important. Failure to develop talent represents a loss of potential wealth which society can not afford. Strang further opines that another important reason for maintenance of good mental health among gifted children is the potential threat they offer to society if their ability is misdirected. Moreover, Strang reports about the reasons for maintaining good mental health.

First, undeveloped talent is expensive to society. It represents a lost contribution.

Second, misdirected ability or talent, as in the case of the criminal or mentally disturbed leader, constitutes a social menace: intelligence and talent can be misused for aggressive, destructive purposes.

Third, the maladjusted individual himself fails to attain the deep satisfaction that accompanies self-fulfilment and service.

It is also stated that perhaps the most important reason for early recognition and guidance of the gifted child is to aid him in attaining the deep satisfaction that accompanies self fulfilment and service.

Martens (1951) finds emotional maladjustment among gifted and recognises this fact by saying that research also shows the danger of emotional maladjustment in individual cases within an unfavourable environment. Prison records tragically reveal those whose giftedness is turned into paths of crime because they were not guided in a desirable fashion. Johnson (1923) and Specht (1919) have observed that teachers' reports revealed gifted children to be above average in many desirable traits, including courtesy, cooperation, willingness to take suggestions and sense of humour. Miller (1957) concluded that social adjustment of the gifted as a group tends to be above average. Even children who have been accelerated in school and are young for their grade placement have been reported as well adjusted. Sociometric studies administered by Gallagher (1958) disclose the fact that the gifted are more frequently chosen by their peers in regular classes. On the other hand Gallagher and Crowder (1957) indicate that on projective tests and rating scales, gifted showed lower frequency of emotional problems. Barbe (1957) and Terman and Oden (1959) report that different types of tests like teachers' ratings, sociometric procedures, personality inventories and projective tests all indicated that gifted had superior emotional stability. It has also been proved that this superiority continues into adulthood. Bonsal and Stefflre (1955) conducted a research working with a group of gifted and a group of non-gifted high school boys. They found the usual pattern of superiority for the gifted as a group. Further, they observed that when gifted and non-gifted students from the same economic levels were compared, little or no differences were found between the two groups. Erikson (1950) has described in detail personality development of gifted children which is given below:

1. *Trust vs. mistrust*: Erikson says that in this area the roots of inner and outer loci of control are found. If as infants, children experience affection and consistency, they form the belief in a secure world wherein they are effective and they matter. If instead their experience is threatening, unpredictable, stressful, or apathetic, they will believe their world to be untrustworthy, unmanageable—one in which they have no control.
2. *Autonomy vs. shame or doubt:* Toddlers who are allowed to feel pride and success in their experiences of learning to care for themselves gain a sense of self-confidence and self-control. If continually limited, criticised, or punished, they will believe themselves to be inadequate or bad and experience shame and self-doubt.
3. *Initiative vs. guilt*: As four to five years olds begin to explore the world beyond themselves, they discover how the world works and how they affect it. If this exploration is challenging and effective, they learn to deal with people and things in

positive ways and gain a strong sense of initiative. If, however, their efforts are always criticised and punished, they feel guilty for self initiated actions.

4. *Industry vs. inferiority:* From six to eleven years of age, children develop numerous skills at home, at school and in the outside world. An evaluation of competence when compared with peers is important at this time. Mistakes must be viewed as growth experiences if further inquiry and exploration are not to be limited.
5. *Ego identity vs. ego diffusion*: The adolescent explores and affirms belief systems and basic values. If all the roles and beliefs found in their lives cannot be resolved into an integrated identity, the result is what Erikson calls ego diffusion.
6. *Intimacy vs. isolation*: In late adolescence and young adulthood the focus is on developing the ability to share one's self with another and still retain the essential self. The success one has in doing this reflects the success of the abovementioned areas of experience.
7. *Generativity vs. self-absorption*: As adults with the problems of earlier stages at least partially resolved, individuals can now direct their focus toward assisting others, one's own children, social issues, etc. Unsuccessful resolution of earlier issues can result in overconcern for one's health, comfort, and psychological needs.
8. *Integrity vs. despair*: As one views one's life from the perspective of age, the evaluation may reflect meaning, purpose and satisfaction or a series of bungled attempts, unresolved efforts, and lost opportunities. The attitude of worth will be affected by this evaluation.

Coleman and Fultz (1985) and Janos and Robinson (1985) have found these children happy and well liked by their peers. They investigated into social and emotional characteristics of gifted and concluded that they play the role of leaders in society. Emotionally, they are well matured and stable. They have positive self-perception, self-sufficient and do not suffer from neurosis and psychosis which displays that they have very sound mental health. However, Lombroso (1905) expressed the views much different from those of Coleman and Fultz (1985) and Janos and Robinson (1985). Lombroso in *The Man of Genius* has written:

> "Just as giants pay a heavy ransom for their stature in sterlity and relative muscular and mental weakness, so the giants of thought expiate their intellectual force in degeneration and psychoses. It is thus that the signs of degeneration are found more frequently in men of genius than even in the insane."

The above statement indicates clearly that highly intellectually gifted or genius people have quite fair chances of having emotional instability or mental diseases which come under the category of neuroticism or psychoticism. In one way Lombroso is right in the sense that very great artists (in any field) sometimes show these symptoms which make clear that they are emotionally not completely fit. The father of psychoanalysis Sigmund Freud also had the view that people of very high intellectual powers and talents sometimes turn away from the norms of the society. The reason is unconscious conflicts, or mental struggle in their own minds. They are not much concerned with the reality of life or real world. But this does not indicate their inefficiency in the field of their own interests. In spite of this deviance their performance is of very high stature in the field of science, music, mathematics, visual or performing art etc. This reminds one of the biography of Edgar Allan Poe by Krutch (1926). Poe was driven to literary eminence by a desire to compensate for a precluded social position, denied sexual craving, and a knowledge of mental instability. The three factors are thought collectively to have effected a strong and persistent drive: "Just as his whole life was a struggle, conducted with all the cunning of the unconscious, against a realisation of the psychic impotence of his sexual nature, so was it a struggle also against a realisation of the mental instability to which the first gave rise." Marks (1925) cites statement by Poe which indicates that he may have had knowledge of his own mental instability:

> "I am come of a race noted for vigour of fancy and ardour of passion. Men have called me mad; but the question is not yet settled, whether much that is glorious, whether all that is profound, does not spring from disease of thought, from

moods of mind enacted at the expense of general intellect."

The example of an English writer Lord Byron is worthmentioning who was an unusual man afflicted with nervous instability. Cassity (1925) states that when Byron was only sixteen years of age he wrote several poems in which he created celestial women who personified the type he most desired. Byron once asserted as follows:

> "I have taken all my fables about the celestial nature of women from the perfection my imagination created in Mary Chatworth (the lady whom he wanted to marry but she refused). I say created, for I found her, like the rest of the sex, anything but angelic." Byron knew his weakness but the experiences in the life led him to become one of the great writers.

Here, I feel it necessary to mention the results of the investigation by Hollingworth (1942) which indicate that these children were not mixed up with their peers. Therefore, they suffered from isolation and as adults also they were not found quite adjusted. But Hallahan and Kauffman (1991) have raised their objection on these results. They remark that the sample of her study was not representative which is clear by her own statement which is as follows:

> "In twenty-three years, seeking in New York City and the local metropolitan area, the densest centre of population in this country and at the same time a great intellectual centre attracting able persons, I have found only twelve children who test at or above 180 IQ (Stanford – Binet). This number represents the winnowing from thousands of children tested, hundreds of them brought for the testing because of their mental gifts."

Very significant point to be noted in her statement is that the sample selected by her was from the category of children of above 180 IQ. Hollingworth found her sample different, may be because of very high level of IQ, *i.e.,* above 180. This type of deviation may not be found among the typically gifted children, *i.e.,* who have 130-150 IQ. Moreover, the extremely intellectually gifted are not easy to find.

Zigler and Farber (1985) have very aptly remarked that to categorise gifted people as those with IQs of 180 or higher is roughly like categorising retarded individuals as only those with IQs of 20 or less. They observe that social and emotional problems may come with children with high IQ. However, White and Renzulli (1987) do not corroborate this view. In fact, gifted do not find the ambience suitable to their mental level. Hence, they are sometimes found maladjusted in schools and at home also. After conducting a survey on gifted children with age range of seven to eighteen years, Galbraith (1985) concluded that these children have certain problems which are not understood by their teachers, parents as well as society members. The problems are as follows:

(*i*) Gifted themselves are not explained the meaning of the term. They think that others keep it very secret.
(*ii*) They are overwhelmed when they succeed in doing the things which they can do.
(*iii*) The school ambience, curriculum, teaching method is unsuitable to them. For them, teachers unnecessarily repeat or explain the subject matter. During that time they have nothing to do in the classroom.
(*iv*) Since they are smarter, they are teased by the classmates.
(*v*) Too much is expected from them by their parents, teachers and others as there is a thinking that they can do everything.
(*vi*) The idea of 'different from others', perplexes them too much and they wish people would accept them what they are.
(*vii*) The problems in the world disturb them. They want to solve them but find unable to do so and this again perplexes them.
(*viii*) Very few friends or people are there who can understand them really.

Though these children most often have many complaints, it has also been found that if parents' dealings with the child are desirable, no doubt, the child is well adjusted even if he has the IQ above 180. Grost (1970) cites an example of a child Mike Grost with an extremely high (over 180) IQ. His mother described him as a happy and gregarious boy who could easily adapt to play with his peers or to social relationship with adults, as the situation demanded. She further described that his wit and charm helped him achieve acceptance among classmates at Michigan State University even at the tender age of ten.

Hollingworth (1926) has found relationship between intellectual ability and character and temperament traits. But Jone and Day (1996) have been of the view that social-emotional characteristics including social aptitudes cannot be predicted on the basis of high ability. Most of the researches have revealed the positive picture of these children so far as their personal and social characteristics are concerned. Gottfried and Gottfried (1996) have reached the conclusion that gifted enjoy to learn, have higher level of persistence and curiosity, quick attention, like to accept challenges and want to study deeply any subject or situation and thus like to get mastery in the field. Ramaseshan (1957) found gifted emotionally better adjusted. Similalry, while compared to children with average intelligence Oram, Dewey and Rutemiller (1995) also found them emotionally highly adjusted in all spheres of life. Cox (1926) and Martinson (1961) have similar ideas on certain points related to these children. Both have found that gifted are much involved in social issues. They like and do also justice. At very early age they develop the ability to know what should be done and what should not be done. They get irritated if some wrong actions are taken by others. Very easily they can differentiate between right and wrong. They have empathy for others and try to solve their problems. Piechwoski (1991) has revealed that they are full of excitement, imagination and emotional reactions. The reason is that they are full of energy. Cassel and Haddox (1959) have opined that gifted play the role of leader in many fields. They find themselves concerned with the problems of others and want to participate in community projects. It has been supported by Roeper (1992) also.

Clark (1979) has proposed the social characteristics of gifted children but these characteristics have been divided mainly into two categories:

1. Differential Societal Characteristics of the Gifted:

(*a*) *Strongly motivated by self-actualisation needs*—Examples of these needs are opportunities to follow divergent paths, pursue strong interests, help in understanding the demands of self-actualisation. But the gifted may have frustration of not feeling challenged and loss of unrealised talents.

(*b*) *Advanced cognitive and affective capacity for conceptualising and solving societal problems*—Special needs are encounters with social problems, awareness of the complexity of problems facing society, conceptual framework for problem–solving procedures. Clark has suggested the possible problems also which these children may have to face. These include the tendency for "quick" solutions not taking into account the complexity of the problem, young age of gifted person often making useable alternatives suspects; older, more experienced decision makers not taking the gifted person seriously.

2. *Differential Social Expectations for the Gifted:*

(*a*) *Leadership Ð*A leader child needs understanding of various leadership steps and practice in leadership skills. Moreover, the child may have the problems like lack of opportunity to use this ability constructively which may result in its disappearance from child's repertoire or its being turned into a negative characteristic, *e.g.*, gang leadership.

(*b*) *Solution to social and environmental problems* – The child wants meaningful involvement in real problems. But the problem may be there such as loss to society if these traits are not allowed to develop with guidance and opportunity for meaningful involvement.

(*c*) *Involvement with the meta-needs of the society* (*e.g., justice, beauty, truth*) – Children who have these characteristics like exploration of the highest levels of human thought; application of this knowledge to today's problems.

Webb (1994) is of the view that these children need freedom of thoughts and actions. They never like to follow others' ideas because they have dominant personality. Gottsfried and Gottsfried (1996) also confirm Webb's findings. Researches conducted by Davis and Rimm (1994) and Freeman (1994) reveal that gifted children never like to make friendship with the children of average intelligence. They prefer the companion of superior intellectual power, no matter that they are older to them in chronological age. Vellerand *et al.* (1994) have observed high level of self-concept and confidence among these children. Hence, they feel themselves superior than their average peers.

This finding has been corroborated by Chan (1996) also. On the other hand Lehman and Erdwins's (1981) investigation led them to conclude that these children appreciate equal treatment with all, help to others and cooperation. They have very high values in their heart for all the values related to humanity. Olszewski-Kubilius *et al.* (1988) made some conclusions after reviewing the previous researches on personality differences between gifted and non-gifted students. The literature revealed that gifted were very well adjusted, had low anxiety and were more responsible. Gifted achievers had more self-control than their underachieving counterparts. Apart from this, gifted males and gifted females were more alike than different on personality profiles. Silverman's (1994) study indicates that gifted show introversion, intensity, perfectionism and sensitivity. Among all these traits, sensitivity plays quite significant role in their life. Due to this particular trait, they at times show the behaviour different from others like immediate reaction to others' behaviour or their feelings also may hurt and they cannot tolerate their own criticism.

Investigators like Vantassel – Baska (1989) and Luftig and Nichols (1991) attempted to know the gender differences. They found that the perceptions held of gifted boys differ significantly from that of gifted girls when rated by their non-gifted, age peers in a heterogeneous school setting. These studies also indicated that gifted boys were given higher status than gifted girls and nongifted boys and girls. They showed popularity, creativity, attractiveness and more skills at sports. But gifted girls were found as least popular, aloof and bossy, placing them at-risk socially among their age peers.

Physical

For a very long time it was believed that gifted are physically weak, not attractive and unimpressive. Their external part of the personality is poor which leads them to be unability to adjust in different spheres of life. The credit goes to scientific studies that put the real picture of these children before us. Martenns (1951) on the basis of a research *Gifted children: What do we know about them? What shall we do about them?* proposed certain physical features of these children. The results of the study revealed that they show on the average high level of physical development, health and mental and social adjustment.

Hollingworth (1942) on the basis of a study of children whose IQ was above 180 concluded that general health was always considered good and that the development of these children was ahead of schedule in all respects. However, the research conducted by Thom and Newell (1945) revealed a different result. It said that a child with high IQ is at his own age level in physical skills and not above it. Olson and Hughes concluded on the basis of a report on the growth patterns of these children that the gifted child is not only superior in intellectual ability but his entire growth pattern is accelerated. It was found that they are taller, weigh more and are stronger than the average children. The investigator remarked that there should be no controversy in this regard. Hollingworth (1926) studied some children with 130 IQ score. The study revealed that the gifted children exceed those of lesser mental ability in height, weight and other physical traits, but that the range within each group overlap. Bentley (1937) after an investigation found that gifted child is usually large and strong for his age and healthier than the average child. A positive correlation was found between size and health of body and intellect in the majority of cases. Though the correlation was not found close but one factor could be inferred from the other in individual cases chosen at random.

The findings of Bentley (1937) are corroborated by Witty (1930) who studied one hundred gifted children. It is revealed by his study that the physical status and general growth of the group was undoubtedly above average. Typically the gifted child was not a physical weakling. He was somewhat above normal in his physical development age. The study also revealed that he approached the normal for the average child more closely in physical traits and motor ability than in mental ability. Witty (1930) researched another group of gifted children for six years and found them to be of better than average bodily development. Witty has stated also a remarkable point that even though the gifted child was superior in physical development, this superiority was not as great as was his mental superiority. Jones (1925) has the view of infrequent physical defects among gifted children. Terman and Witty (1930) studied the health histories of gifted children and found that the general physical health of both the child and his parents was better than average. Children were slightly heavier at birth. They cut their first tooth about two months earlier and walked and talked about two months earlier than the average child. It was also observed that these children were more precocious in speech development than they were in other areas. Later development seemed to follow an accelerated programme and pubescence was reached earlier by the gifted. Usually, it was thought that children with brilliance were, frail and weak but these two investigators rejected this concept as they found that these children were healthy, large and robust. Physical defects were found less frequently among them than among unselected population. They were in general fine physical specimens who enjoyed good growth and health. Miles (1954) opined that as a group, the gifted tend to exceed the average on measures of physical traits. Burks, Jensen and Terman (1930) have reported that a study of Terman's gifted group showed them to have superior ratings on thirty-four anthropometric measures, including height, weight and general physical development. Monahan and Hollingworth (1927) have reported superior neuromuscular capacity among children of superior intelligence.

The results of the longitudinal study conducted by Terman and his associate (1947) reveal that the gifted children as a group were above the best standards for American-born children in growth status as indicated by both height and weight. The study further shows that the gifted group was slightly superior physically to the various groups used for comparison. This comprehensive and quite exhaustive study rejects the idea that gifted are weakling, unable to compete with their classmates in any area other than intelligence. Terman and Oden (1959) followed gifted children, identified earlier, into middle age and found that they maintained their superior physical characteristics. They were found to be larger at birth, earlier in achieving physical development milestones such as walking, healthier, outstanding athletic ability, superior competitors and less anxious than average children. On the whole they were judged to be physically superior by the investigators. Here one has to be careful that there exists a positive relationship between intelligence and socio-economic status. The findings by Terman and Oden may have the influence of this factor. But Laycock and Caylor (1964) made an attempt to compare siblings with widely varying IQs. The results revealed no significant differences on measures of physical variables. But sometimes it has also been seen that people with superior intellectual abilities do not have superior body built which may lead them toward inferiority complex in certain areas of life.

Clark (1979) has discussed in detail the physical characteristics of gifted children which are presented below:

1. Unusual quantity of input from the environment through a heightened sensory awareness:

The examples of related needs are: to engage in activities that will allow integration and assimilation of sensory data. Concomitant problems may be attention moving diffusely toward many areas of interests: over expenditure of energy due to lack of integration; seeming disconnectedness.

2. Unusual discrepancy between physical and intellectual development:

Example may be to appreciate their physical capacities. Concomitant problems are the result in gifted adults who function with a mind/body dichotomy; gifted children who are only comfortable expressing themselves in mental activity resulting in a limited development both physically and mentally.

3. Low tolerance for the lag between their standards and their athletic skills:

Example may be to discover physical activities as a source of pleasure; to find satisfaction in small increments of improvement; to engage in non-competitive physical activities. Concomitant problems are to refuse to take part in any activities where they do not excel; limiting their experience with otherwise pleasurable, constructive physical activities.

4. "Cartesian split" – can include neglect of physical well-being and avoidance of physical activity:

Examples of related needs are: to engage in activities leading to mind/body integration; to develop a commitment to own physical well-being; to extend this concern to the social and political realm. Possible problems are detrimental to full mental and physical health, inhibiting to the development of potential for the individual.

Family Background and Socio-Economic Status

In general, gifted are considered to belong to the family of above average status in all respects. There is a common belief that such a child is the first child in the family and also the family is small. Goddard's (1928) study has indicated half as being first born and three fourths as being either first or second born. Of the first born, forty five out of a total of 253 subjects were the only children. Hollingworth (1926) on the basis of her research concluded that gifted children had few siblings. With respect to the order of birth, more than half of the subjects were first born. Terman (1940) reported that the parents of the gifted subjects had produced an average of 3.09 (children) per family. Barbe (1956) in a study attempted to determine the size of the family and the order of birth of the gifted child. About 21.8 per cent of the subjects had no siblings, while 42.6 per cent had only one. Almost 20 per cent had two siblings and seven per cent three. About 22 per cent of the subjects in Barbe's study were the only children. About 29 per cent were second born and only 9.3 third born. The data indicated that in the group the gifted children were the first born in a family having two children. Barbe concluded that eighty seven and a half per cent of the gifted subjects were reared by their own parents. The next largest group, *i.e.,* 7.2 per cent were reared by only their mothers. 2 per cent were reared by their own mother and a step father, and 1.5 per cent by their own father and a step mother. The father or foster parents each reared 0.9 per cent of the total number of subjects. Witty (1940) selected one hundred gifted children to study and found that most of their parents were American born. But the situation was quite different in the study conducted by Barbe (1956). Slightly less than fifty per cent of the subjects had one or both parents who were foreign born.

So far as educational level of the parents of gifted children is concerned Hollingworth (1926) has remarked that the educational level of the parents of gifted subjects was far above the average for their generation. In the majority of the cases where the gifted child had been born since 1915, both parents were graduates of high school, and in far more cases than in the population at large both parents were college graduates. Terman (1925) found that gifted had parents whose average formal education exceeded that of the general population by four or five years. More often the parents had graduated from college and received doctorate degree. On the other hand Barbe (1956) observes that of the fathers of the subjects, 38.4 per cent had a grammar school education or less, 33.6 per cent had a high school education, 8.8 per cent trade or business school, and 19.2 per cent had some college education. Of the mothers of the subjects, 32.5 per cent had a grammar school education or less, 42.2 per cent had a high school education, 12.3 per cent trade or business school, and 13.0 per cent had some college education. The mothers of the gifted subjects on the average appeared to be slightly better educated than the fathers through the high school and business school levels. However, there were more fathers than mothers who attended college.

In the field of occupation, Cole (1956) has found that many researches reveal that parents of gifted children are found more frequently among professional and managerial group. Barbe (1956) listed the occupations of the parents according to the U.S. census classification. The Dictionary of Occupational Titles was used to classify the occupations into seven distinct groups:

(*i*) Professional and managerial
(*ii*) Clerical and sales
(*iii*) Service
(*iv*) Agriculture, fishery, forestry etc.
(*v*) Skilled
(*vi*) Semi-skilled
(*vii*) Unskilled.

The subjects were asked the title and description of the father's occupation. It was possible to classify all but a few of the occupations listed where descriptions were not given and two classifications were possible, the data were omitted. Classifications of the parent's occupation were made for four hundred and thirty seven subjects. Three of the remaining nineteen were on government pensions while rest gave no response to the question at all. The following table depicts the same:

Occupational Level of Parents of Gifted Subjects

Professional and managerial	40.3%
Clerical and sales	22.4%
Service	3.7%
Agriculture, fishery, forestry etc.	0.2%
Skilled	21.5%
Semi-skilled	8.2%
Unskilled	3.7%

Terman (1925) found 81.4 per cent subjects whose parents' occupational status was of the rank of professional, semi-professional or business while only 6.8 per cent had parents who belonged to the category of semi-skilled and unskilled labour. Hollingworth (1926) reached the result that more than fifty per cent of the children testing above 140 IQ had fathers who were professional men or proprietors. It was also found that half of the remaining fathers were in semi-professional and clerical occupations. Parents' occupational status has been found positively correlated with the academic achievement of gifted subjects. Cattell and Brimhall (1921) revealed that 43.1 per cent of the fathers of 885 leading American scientists came from among the professions. Clarke (1916) had reported that the same was true for the fathers of 49.2 per cent of 666 American men of letters.

Regarding family environment Stouffer and Shea (1959) have observed that the home environment of gifted subjects was found more stimulating than the average. The families tended to be less autocratic, read more and better books and magazines, travelled more and in general had greater energy and stability. They further found that the cultural patterns of the families tended to encourage education and achievement. Havighurst (1962) is of the view that the upper and upper-middle classes, jointly produce nearly twice as many children with IQs in the top quartile as are produced by the average family, and less than one-half as many children in the lowest quartile.

So far as marital status and divorce rate of the gifted childrens' parents are concerned, Terman's (1947) study reveals that until 1922, 5.2 per cent of the parents of his gifted group had been divorced and 1.9 per cent were separated. By 1940, the percentage of divorced and separated parents had risen to 13.9. But Barbe (1956) found that eighty per cent of the parents of the subjects were living together while the subject was in public school. The remaining five per cent consists of cases where one or both of the parents were deceased.

School achievement is positively related to the family status. Similarly cultural factors also play a significant role in school performance. Burt (1962) says that cultural factors play an important role in the sphere of school life. Bond (1957) remarks that the importance of general cultural influence on achievement and on opportunity is indicated by the fact that a librarian's son is one thousand times more likely to win a National Merit Scholarship than is a labourer's son.

Renzulli (1973) has emphasised on the research related to the socio-economic status of these children. The investigation conducted by Frierson (1965) will not be out of place if mentioned here; he found that upper status gifted children were aware of parental aspirations for their college education while it was not found in the case of many lower status gifted. Lower status gifted did not like school as well, read as much or achieved as highly in science as the upper-status gifted; competitive team sports were preferred more by lower status gifted than by upper status gifted. Upper status gifted children were superior to the lower status gifted group in the area of creative potential.

Psychological

Intellectual

The most important criterion of identifying giftedness is intelligence quotient. In general, the cut off point used is an IQ score that is at least two standard deviations above average. This would indicate that the individual scores higher than approximately ninety eight per cent of the population. Since most intelligence tests have a standard deviation of 15, this means a person would have an IQ of 130 or better (Taylor and Sternberg, 1989). It is necessary to know here that there are a number of cognitive or mental abilities. Right from the beginning, on the basis of deviant behaviour (result of superiority in cognition), parents can understand that their child is mentally different from others. This can happen only if parents and other family members are themselves intelligent enough and well aware of the behaviour of the child. But unfortunately if parents are unable to understand the reality of the child, the ability of the child is not cared for and the child faces maltreatment which is psychologically very injurious and damaging as well. Only the words Superior Mental Ability do not speak all about the gifted population. At this point, it is necessary to know how and in what way these children differ from their peers with normal intelligence. To quote Baker (1949) will be most relevant in this regard; he emphasised that two important areas need to be considered – the quantitative and qualitative characteristics of mental superiority.

Quantitative Differences in Intelligence

The superior learner has a surplus mental age beyond his chronological life age. This surplus begins as soon as he is born, and by the time he reaches six years of age, his increased ratio of mental growth has produced at least one year of mental maturity above his age.

Qualitative Differences in Intelligence

There are two qualitative differences in intelligence:

(a) Superior learners tend to learn by complex associative methods rather than by simple, direct rote drill. By such associative processes, they are able to make many connections or to use many mental facets upon which they may draw when putting meaning into learning.
(b) A second qualitative characteristic is that superior children look for the abstract or generalised rules underlying all school subjects.

This shows that a gifted child is superior in both quantitative as well as qualitative intelligences. The knowledge of these two becomes more important when the child is admitted to a school. It is not necessary that only an intelligence test will guide us to decide whether a child is gifted. Through general behaviour of the child also, one can know about the giftedness of the child. The only need is the mental alertness and awareness of the parents, family members and teachers as well. Terman (1925) found the following intellectual characteristics of gifted children:

1. One in five skipped part or all of first grade.
2. Nearly half could read before entering kindergarten.
3. They averaged forty per cent higher scores than age-mates on tests of achievement, with the largest differences in the areas of reading, arithmetic reasoning, literature, science, the arts and general information. Small differences were found in spelling, historical facts and arithmetic computations.
4. Gifted finished school earlier than children with normal intelligence.
5. They read more and better books, had many hobbies and made numerous collections.
6. They were generally well rounded in their achievement and interests.

Some other researchers like Witty (1930), Hollingworth (1942), Cox (1926), Carrol (1940), Witty (1940), Martinson (1972), Gallagher and Crowder (1957) and Parkyn (1948) have supported the views expressed by Terman. It has been reported by Terman and Oden (1947) that parents can recognise the child on the basis of curiosity, quick understanding, good grasping power, extensive information, retentive memory, large vocabulary and unusual interest in such things as number relations etc. Hollingworth (1926) concluded that very early interest and ability in reading are signs of superior intelligence. Further she stated that in the opinions of their teachers, pupils selected as bright were more inquisitive, more imaginative, more courteous and had a keener sense of humour than the average child. Carrol's (1940) view is that gifted children are characterized by early development of self-criticism, initiative and independence in thinking, ability to see relationships, make associations, adapt abstract principles to concrete situations, and observe and remember details. It is further reported by him that the gifted child is superior in such traits as desire to know, desire to excel, originality, and power to learn.

William, *et al.* (1951) after administering an intelligence test, reported about the abilities possessed by mentally superior children such as high degree of general intelligence, the ability to do abstract thinking and other types of relational thinking. These children are high in respect of the general intelligence factor which Spearman designated by the letter 'g'. In terms of Thurstone's theory they possess to a high degree most, if not all, of the eight primary mental abilities. It is further stated that the mentally gifted are characterised by 'power' – that is, they are able to do mental tasks of a high degree of difficulty. The mentally gifted are alert and quick. They are also characterised by broad attention-span, by a high degree of insight into problems, and by the ability to generalise. Goodhart and Schmidt (1940) have stated that gifted have great curiosity, wide range of divergent interests, a large, fluid vocabulary, good memory, the ability to generalise, interpret and recognise relationships, the ability to use economy in work methods and a strong sense of responsibility.

The researchers have also reported the areas in which gifted are not superior which is quite interesting to know. They show carelessness in the mechanics of spelling, punctuation and computation. Needless to mention that there exists a high and positive correlation between IQ and achievement scores. Terman and Oden (1947) found that the achievement quotients (AQ) of the gifted subjects were not equally high in all subjects. They found that the superiority of gifted over unselected children was greatest in reading, language usage, arithmetical reasoning, and information in science, literature and the arts. Their superiority was less marked in arithmetical computation, spelling, and factual information about history and civics. In the subjects like penmanship, manual training, sewing and cooking, these children did not perform much better than did unselected children. Further, both the researchers found minor achievement differences between gifted boys and girls in various subjects, but these sex differences were of little value when compared with the great superiority of gifted over unselected children. Hence, they concluded that the amount of unevenness in the subject matter profiles of gifted children does not differ significantly from that shown in the profiles of unselected children. It was also found that the unevenness of the gifted child occurred on a higher level of achievement than that of the normal child on a much lower level.

The studies by some investigators (Hollingworth, 1926; and Witty, 1930) have rejected the notion that giftedness does not continue throughout the life. Moreover, Terman and Oden (1947) retested the children, studied earlier, later in life. It was found that the intellectual status of the average member of the group at the mean age of thirty years was close to the 98th or 99th percentile of the general adult population, and was far above the average level of ability of graduates from superior colleges and universities. Frank and Dolan (1982) found gifted children having advanced logical thinking, such as ability of how to question and problem solving behaviour while Davis and Rimm's (1985) investigation reveals that these children have precocity in the field of language. Moreover, Brown and Yakimowski (1987) have concluded that students who were gifted, showed a qualitatively different pattern of subtest scores on an intelligence test compared with both students with average intelligence and students with above average intelligence scores who were not considered gifted. Kitano and Kirby (1986) administered checklists for measuring intellectual abilities of gifted children. They found that these children have the characteristics of rapid learning, advanced vocabulary, the ability to generalise quickly from principles, long attention span, a tendency to become bored with routine types of tasks and good retention of information. Laycock (1979), Maker (1986), Clark (1988) and Maker and Schiever (1989) have summarised the common intellectual characteristics on the basis of their researches. These are as follows:

A gifted child:

- Generalizes learning
- Reasons abstractly
- Can show unevenness
- Conceptualises
- Remembers great amount of material
- Processes information well
- Displays high level of verbal ability
- Dislikes drill and routine
- Shows intellectual curiosity
- Learns quickly
- Has wide interests
- Solves problems.

There has been a controversy on the tests which help identifying the characteristics of gifted children. The Scholastic Aptitude Test (SAT) was studied in detail and analysed by the Commission on Tests in 1970. The commission was not fully satisfied and reported that

SAT was too narrow in judging the probability of students' success in college. It was found that SAT was able to test only verbal reasoning abilities and mathematics well while some more skills also are included in high potential. On the other hand Renzulli (1973) suggested that the test administered to measure the intelligence of gifted children should have certain characteristics and the test should be able to highlight whether gifted students are able to show these characteristics:

(*i*) The child is able to manage, process and use information meaningfully.
(*ii*) He is able to adapt easily to new learning ambience.
(*iii*) The gifted's level of motivation is very high.
(*iv*) He is able to express himself in different areas like writing, art, oral expressions, non-verbal expressions and expressions through graphic pictures.
(*v*) The child has good work habits and a high degree of task involvement under varying conditions.
(*vi*) The child comprehends the meaning of different information gathered in different manners – like listening, experiencing, looking and reading.
(*vii*) He can use non-standard pools of information.
(*viii*) Demonstrates abilities to search out, analyse and synthesise information.
(*ix*) Solves problems in situations that require varied reasoning as well as thinking.

Hallahan and Kauffman (1991) have reported that intellectual precocity has been recognised throughout recorded history. Clark (1979) has explained the cognitive abilities, examples of related needs and possible concomitant problems which gifted children show through their behaviour. They are like this:

Extraordinary Quantity of Information, Unusual Retentiveness

Examples these needs are: to be exposed to new and challenging information of the environment and the culture including aesthetic, economic, political, educational and social aspects; to acquire early mastery of foundation skills. Possible related problems are boredom with regular curriculum; impatience with "waiting for the group."

Advanced Comprehension

Access to challenging curriculum and intellectual peers may be the related needs. Poor interpersonal relationships with less able children of the same age; adults considering child "Sassy" or "smart alec", a dislike for repetition of already understood concepts are the concomitant problems.

Unusually Varied Interests and Curiosity

Examples of these needs are: to be exposed to varied subjects and concerns; to be allowed to pursue individual ideas. The problems related are difficult in conforming to group tasks; overextending energy levels, taking on too many projects at one time.

High Level of Language Development

The gifted may have the needs to encounter uses for increasingly difficult vocabulary and concepts. Possible related problem may be that the child is perceived as a "show off" by children of the same age.

High Level of Verbal Ability

The child may need to share ideas verbally in depth. He may have the problems, such as trying to dominate discussions with information and questions deemed negative by teachers and fellow students; use of verbalism to avoid difficult thinking tasks.

Unusual Capacity for Processing Information

The child needs to be exposed to ideas at many levels and in large variety. Related problems may be resentment if interrupted; perceived as too serious; dislike for routine and drill.

Accelerated Pace of Thought Processes

Needs are: to be exposed to ideas at rates appropriate to individual pace to learning. The gifted may have frustration with inactivity and absence of progress.

Flexible Thought Processes

The gifted needs to be allowed to solve problems in diverse ways. The problem before such a child is that he is seen as disruptive and disrespectful to authority and tradition.

Comprehensive Synthesis

The gifted needs to be allowed a longer incubation time for ideas. Possible problems are frustration with demands for deadlines, and for completion of each level prior to starting new inquiry.

Early Ability to Delay Closure

Related needs are: the child should be allowed to pursue ideas and integrate new ideas without forced closure or demanded products. Possible concomitant problems if products are demanded as proof of learning are that he will refuse to pursue an otherwise interesting subject or line of inquiry.

Heightened Capacity for Seeing Unusual and Diverse Relationship

The child has the need to mess around with varieties of materials and ideas. There is a possibility of frustration at being considered "off the subject" or irrelevant in pursuing enquiry in areas other than the subject being considered; considered odd or weired by others.

Ability to Generate Original Ideas and Solutions

Related needs are to build skills in problem solving and productive thinking, opportunity to contribute to solution to meaningful problems. The child may feel difficulty with rigid conformity; may be penalised for not following directions; may deal with rejection by becoming rebellious.

Early Differential Patterns for Thought Processing (e.g., Thinking in Alternatives, Abstract Terms, Sensing Consequences, Making Generalizations)

Examples of related needs are: to be exposed to alternatives, abstractions, consequences of choices and opportunities for drawing generalisations and testing them. Possible concomitant problems are rejection or omission of detail; questions generalisations of others which may be perceived as disrespectful behaviour.

Early Ability to Use and Form Conceptual Frameworks

Needs related to this characteristic are: to use and to design conceptual frameworks in information gathering and problem solving; to seek order and consistency; to develop tolerance for ambiguity. The child may have the problems of frustration with inability of others to understand or appreciate original organisations or insights; personally devised systems or structure may conflict with procedures or systems later taught.

An Evaluative Approach to Themselves and Others

Examples of related needs are: to be exposed to individuals of varying ability and talent, and to varying ways of seeing and solving problems; to set realistic achievable short-term goals; to develop skills in data evaluation and decision making.

Persistent, Goal Directed Behaviour

The gifted may have the need to be allowed to pursue inquiries beyond allotted time spans, to set and evaluate priorities. The possible problems are that the child may be perceived as stubborn, wilfull and uncooperative.

Suffice to say that though gifted children can be recognised by their parents and other family members on the basis of their behaviour like insatiable curiosity, keenness for information, asking too many questions, quick learning, good grasping power, precocity in different areas etc., but testing of cognitive abilities is very important for identifying these children.

Adjustment

There is a misconception that a gifted child has no adjustment problems. It is not absolutely true in all the cases. However the early researches by Terman (1925), Witty (1930) and Hollingworth (1942) dispelled the beliefs that the gifted are "the products of supernatural causes of human behaviour," and that "intellectual precocity is pathological." All these researchers found the gifted to be physically superior, attractive, and generally well adjusted. Grotberg (1965) has observed that although it has been recognised that adjustment problems existed among gifted, relatively little effort was made to investigate problem behaviour. However, Hollingworth (1942) found that pupils of IQ's 180 plus had more adjustment problems than pupils whose IQ's fell between 130 and 180. Haggard (1957) found that by third grade high achievers responded to socialisation pressures and accepted adult values readily. It was also found that they cooperated, had good work habits and maintained satisfactory relationship with parents, peers and teachers. They were also highly competitive in nature. Gowan (1955) concluded that underachievers frequently experienced parental rejection and hostility. On the other hand O'Leary (1955) found underachievers in the ninth grade to have poor work habits. Roesslein (1953) remarked that there existed a pattern involving over solicitous parents and resultant feelings of inadequacy among high school male underachievers. Patterns of maladjustment found among underachievers at the college level by Wedemeyer (1953) and Horrall (1957) were similar to those noted in the elementary and high school pupils. Armstrong (1955) studied the adjustment of underachievers in the ninth and eleventh grades and concluded that they were more influenced by the desires of others rather than their own wishes and were regarded by their teachers as uncooperative, undependable, and poor in judgement. Similarly Shaw and Brown (1957) found a high degree of hostility and hypercritical attitudes among underachieving college students.

Grotberg (1965) expressed the views that there are two methods of identifying the maladjustment among gifted:

(*a*) Underachievement in elementary, high school and college.
(*b*) To study gifted adults who have been institutionalised and whose conditions have been diagnosed. These individuals are to a large extent the underachievers or failures as adults. Grotberg selected forty gifted and forty non-gifted institutionalised patients as experimental and control groups respectively. Each group contained twenty male and twenty female patients. The gifted population was selected on the basis of high IQ. An IQ of 120 was set as the base, and the

range was from 120 to 137. An IQ between 80 and 110 was used to designate the non-gifted population. Wechsler-Bellevue or Adult Intelligence Scale, the Rorschach Test, a Thematic Apperception Test, and a sentence completion examination were administered to ascertain the characteristics which differentiated the gifted population from the non-gifted population. The investigator summarised the characteristics as follows:

The institutionalised gifted resembled the age groups of the institutionalised non-gifted and developed no higher set of controls to ward off or postpone a psychotic or psychoneurotic disorder. The adjustment advantage found among gifted children and youth is apparently lost in adulthood. The institutionalised gifted was better educated than the non-gifted. The gifted male continued higher education more frequently than the gifted female at a rate of more than two to one. The gifted male also continued higher education for more advanced degrees than the gifted female. Gifted males had the better occupational positions and had the higher socio-economic status. Gifted females attained no higher socio-economic status than the non-gifted. The institutionalised gifted male tended to become schizophrenic and to display paranoid or obsessive compulsive features. He was more likely to project the blame for his failure onto others. He was not so likely to assume responsibility for his own failure. The gifted female more frequently developed psychoneurotic disorders. Further it was also found that the gifted male was more frequently aware of his superiority and also of his own sense of failure. Neither the gifted male nor female had marked positive attitudes towards work; indeed their attitudes were highly negative. Both the gifted male and female tended to reject pressure in terms of parental expectations. Yet as a group, they submitted to parental pressure about as frequently as did the non-gifted population. However, they more frequently attempted to surpass the expectations and achievements of their parents.

The abovementioned researches indicate that some gifted people find themselves unable to accept others' thoughts and ideas easily as there is a difference between their and others' mental level. It becomes the responsibility of parents as well as teachers to make these children learn to accept the environment and themselves also with the uniqueness. Cross (1997) has remarked that the positive social and emotional growth of gifted children is more related to how well the environment responds to and provides for their needs than to the different characteristics they present. In the absence of positive responses from others, gifted develop negative characteristics like they try to hide their high abilities so that others do not assess them as mentally superior (Davis and Rimm, 1994). This results in the non use of intellectual powers which is quite damaging as well as psychologically injurious to them. This leads them to the situation of confusion as they are at times undecided whether to show their ability or not. In the classroom also the whole ambience for them is not interesting and likeable rather it bores them. Besides, the peers also tease them and comment that they are over smart as all the answers come from these children in the classroom which irritates other students. Researchers like Hollingworth (1942) and Tennenbaum (1983) have observed that the more highly gifted the child, the greater the risk for social-emotional maladjustment and unhappiness. Leaverton and Herzog (1979) conducted a study to judge the overall adjustment of highly gifted children. The investigators noted that very low priority was given to the problems of this group. Of the 113 children tested, only 13 were seen by the school psychologist and these 13 had been referred for the sole purpose of testing. Apart from this Roedell's (1984) investigation has revealed eight areas of vulnerability of which to be aware so that these risks can be minimized:

(*i*) Perfectionism
(*ii*) Uneven development
(*iii*) Role conflicts
(*iv*) Self definition
(*v*) Inappropriate environments
(*vi*) Adult expectations
(*vii*) Alienation and
(*viii*) Intense sensitivity

Further, Roedell observed that the most frequent symptom among gifted population has been found to be lack of confidence, resulting in a helpless orientation toward perceived failure. When this interacts with heightened perfectionism, ineffective problem solving and increasingly lowered self-concept are found. Roedell opined that these problems can be alleviated.

Barbe's (1954) investigation has revealed very interesting results. It was found that gifted children tend to choose one of three patterns of adjustment with their world: They may choose to withdraw, to isolate themselves from the group; this occurs most often when the situation offers no challenge. They may become the class clown, showing off in an effort to be accepted and to gain favourable attention; this behaviour may be carried to the point that teachers and the peer group reject such attempts as being inappropriate or silly, or they may view the child as a nuisance. Barbe said that finally gifted children may seek conformity through pleasing others or by pretending not to know answers in an effort to seem like everyone else, to hide a superior intellect; this dangerous game of non-use may result in loss of function—growth cannot be nurtured through this subterfuge. It was also concluded that in this way, gifted children may find themselves becoming role players or what our educational system calls "underachievers." Barbe has pointed out a very sensitive and significant issue, *i.e.,* underachievement among gifted. This is the most serious problem which restricts these children to contribute in any sphere of their life and society as well. It is one of the important negative techniques of coping up with the rest of the society. It has been proved by Webb (1994) and Cross (1997). These researchers are of the view that drop out rate for gifted students may now be as high as twenty per cent of the total number of students who drop out of high school. One very significant problem among these children has been found, *i.e.,* the suicide. It is quite alarming as it is growing in incidence. While investigating in detail about suicide, Cross (1997) has found it as the second leading cause of death among adolescents, with ten per cent of all adolescents making such attempts.

Newland (1976) has cautioned the whole society that we should assure the gifted that we are concerned with their social interaction with others, not just their social adjustment to others. This may help this group in adjustment. Higham and Buescher (1987) and Silverman (1991) have suggested if gifted students are placed in classes that allow them to interact with mental peers, value their mental ability, and provide for appropriate educational challenges, their social-emotional relationships as well as their intellectual growth flourish. If given the chance and opportunity, gifted have the ability to adjust, through different strategies. One of them which is very important is to engage them in cocurricular activities in the school. Catharsis as well as full utilisation of their intellect is quite possible through these activities. Cross (1997) has been in favour of these activities as they help reducing tension, stress and excess of anxiety. It is also suggested by Cross that it is important to create opportunities for these children to spend time together.

So it becomes very necessary, that the most suitable and congenial environment alongwith guidance and counselling at home as well as school should be provided, if the society intends to harness their extra potentials and intellectual abilities.

Perfectionism

Gifted have high expectations from themselves, hence they are very careful about the deeds done by them. They always wish whatever they do, should be perfect in all respects. The belief in ideal performance may be unrealistic. But even then they try to do the work without shortcoming. Cross (1997) opines that though every individual likes perfection but these children are more perfectionist which is not possible if desired in total form. This impossibility sometimes may lead them to frustration and depression which directly takes them toward maladjustment. But one may ask, why they get frustrated if they are unable to touch perfection point? The answer is that they are expected to do each and every type of task and that too perfectly. This high expectation creates fear of failure in their heart. This develops mental pressure and demand from others also. Greenspon (2000) has very aptly observed that this is the fundamental problem with perfectionism, under this belief, one can never feel good enough to be acceptable as a person. Pressing oneself to do better is healthy; feeling that one must be either perfect or worthless is not.

The Crux of the problem is that these children expect perfection from others also. The basis of their friendship with others also includes this particular characteristic which affects the interrelationships in an adverse fashion. If they are not made clear of the reality, this may go throughout their life. Buffington (1987) has concluded that not only is the perfectionist less productive but also perfectionism contributes to moodiness, relationship problems, loneliness, and limited self-acceptance. Certain suggestions have been given by him following which the gifted child can be taught about dealing with the problem such as:

- The child needs to be taught to learn from his own mistakes.
- The knowledge of gains and losses of being a perfectionist should be made clear to the child. Also the extent of perfection needs clarity before the child.
- How to separate a number of thoughts from others should be in the knowledge of the child. This will help him a lot in gaining success in life.
- The child should be encouraged to celebrate the success even if it is quite small for him as this helps changing the mood and remove monotony in his life.
- The child needs to learn and know the level of self-acceptance. He should try to maintain a balanced self-acceptance.

Lack of balanced feeling for perfection takes the child toward excessive anxiety. The child rates himself/herself as worthless in the world. Starts to suffer from ineffective coping strategies. Feels as if he will not be able to do anything in a desirable manner. No doubt, that perfectionism most of the time helps developing low self-worth and self-esteem, and dissatisfaction among these children. But this does not mean that this concept needs to be removed from the mind of these children. The need is to pay attention and care on this attribute. Parker and Adkins (1995) suggest that perfectionism needs attention and alternative coping strategies, acknowledging the positive aspects of the pursuit of excellence seems to necessitate perseverance, high standards, extraordinary effort and maximum use of talent.

It may be asked why the feeling of perfection takes birth in the mind of the gifted. Among the significant reasons, the child himself rates very high in all respects; this can be called as high expectations from the child himself. Secondly, excess of praise the child receives from all the corners of the society including parents and teachers.

Repetetion of praise sometimes may become psychologically injurious to the child. As a result of all time praises the child may start to depend and may expect it again and again. But a time comes when its repetition is not felt necessary, this hurts the child and may take toward undesirable personality development. Davis and Rimm (1994) support this view. In fact, to save these children from psychological trauma, there is a need to provide frequent guidance and counselling services so that they can stop themselves from going to the path of unrealistic world and remove themselves from the most ideal situations which are not completely possible for a human being on this planet. They need to know the reality of life and practicality also. This may reduce their tension and worries to some extent and they may lead a life like others in the society.

Intrinsic Motivation

Gifted do not need and like extrinsic motivation as they are full of intrinsic motivation. No need to compel to make them sit for studies and other activities. They themselves are always busy in the subject of their interest. They have insatiable curiosity, like challenges, have self-determination for any task, inner strength and capability to do the task, committed to achieve the set goal. Amabile (1989) and Gottfried and Gottfried (1996) have observed that students with intrinsic motivation are satisfied with their efforts irrespective of the opinions of others, and are found to have lower academic anxiety. Collahan (1981) observes that the distinguishing characteristics of motivation and perseverance were noted above and as part of Renzulli's definition of giftedness. These factors among others, were noted by Terman and his followers among the characteristics of the successful gifted adults. These studies have produced some retrospective evidence of the characteristics of intellectually gifted individuals that have led to satisfaction, success, and occupational persistence as adults. A follow up survey was conducted by Sears (1977) to compare the most successful and less successful individuals from the original sample of Terman. The results of the survey revealed that occupational satisfaction and work persistence were best predicted by feelings of satisfaction, ambition (achievement motivation), and good health as early as age thirty.

It is quite obvious that the child with intrinsic motivation in the field of studies achieves very high. Hence, need is felt to enhance instrinsic motivation. Lashaway-Bokina (2000) opined that elimination of overt supervision, flexible deadlines, stimulating environment, choice, and minimal competitions help in this regard. School ambience including curriculum may help a lot enhancing this motivation. Gottfried and Gottfried (1996) are in favour of specially designed curriculum for these children. Researches have revealed that maintenance of intrinsic motivation does not require external rewards (Edwards, 1997) rather it is devastating.

Morality and Ethics

Usually it is thought that giftedness, goes with morality and ethical values. Unintentionally we expect from the gifted that he/she has to be a moralist, believer in justice and democracy and must be having very high levels of values existing in the society. On the whole these expectations are not entirely wrong. Most of the gifted prove themselves right on these expectations. Terman (1926) and Hollingworth (1942) through their studies have proved that these children right from very early age start to show the symptoms of ethics and morality. They have the ability to know about justice and injustice, right and wrong, good and bad while all these concepts are abstract in nature. They are not only the believer of these values rather they implement them in their own life also which takes them toward idealism. Galbraith (1985) has also corroborated the findings by Terman and Hollingworth. Gallagher (1985) has observed that most studies' results reveal that gifted believe in moral as well as ethical values to a high degree.

We should also have the knowledge that like other developments moral and ethical development also takes place agewise or it can be said that this development differs from one stage to another one. Kohlberg (1984) has drawn the conclusions on the basis of longitudinal studies conducted on 50 individuals for about 20 years of time. The word moral development has been used in the studies which is being presented like this:

Infancy Period

Stage one: Authority figures dictate the child's actions. Children follow moral rules to avoid punishment. During the first five to eight years of life, most children find this belief reinforced regularly.

Childhood period: It has two stages

Stage two: The child gradually becomes aware of the ideas of reciprocity: "If I do something for you, you will do something for me." There is concern for rewards: "What is in it for me?" Throughout both these stages, which generally continue through the primary grades, the emphasis is on external control and on concrete consequences.

Stage three: The child seeks to meet the expectations of others, being a "good" child. Being "nice" is now seen in a broader context. The ability to see situations from the position of other persons helps determine the action a child will take.

Adolescence Period

Stage four: Concern for others now encompasses more of society. The law, rules of the social system, and a desire to do one's duty gain consideration. Avoidance of guilt and social disapproval motivate the child. Kohlberg estimated that only ten per cent of the adult population goes beyond this externally controlled level of development.

Adulthood Period

Stage five: The maturity of internal commitment to principles of one's own conscience develops. At this stage, responsibility, the rights of others, and human dignity are also truly understood. Avoidance of self-condemnation is now important.

Source: Barbara Clark: *Growing up gifted* (6th ed.), New Jersey, Merrill Prentice Hall, 2002.

Kohlberg has indicated no difference between moral development of gifted belonging to different cultures, socio-economic status, social classes and boys and girls. Here we need to be cautious about the individual differences among gifted. The reason is that some gifted may divert their potential toward criminal or destructive activities. Hallahan and Kauffman (1991) remark that the corruptibility of major figures in every profession, in every society raises questions about the moral and ethical superiority of gifted children.

Self-concept

Abraham Maslow has contributed a lot in the field of self-concept. Basically there are two categories of self concepts:

(*a*) Intellectual or academic self-concept: The gifted child is very high in this type of self-concept. It is the base of giftedness. The child estimates himself/herself quite high.
(*b*) Social self-concept: It is concerned with the social approval of the gifted by others as well as himself/herself.

Researches have revealed that in comparison to social self-concept, gifted have been found having higher academic or intellectual self-concept (Silverman, 1991). Davis and Rimm (1994) and Colangelo (1991) support the view and observe that some of the gifted may have quite low social self concept. Maslow has talked about self-actualisation in much detail. He proposed hierarchy of needs of an individual. This hierarchy is like this:

Transcendence
Self-actualisation
Self-esteem needs
Love and Belongingness needs
Security/Safety needs
Physiological/basic needs

Maslow explained all these needs. The meeting of needs starts from the lowest level. Only after meeting lower side's needs, the individual goes to upper sides' needs' fulfilment. If any lower level need is not met, one cannot go to meet remaining needs. The individual has to touch each step of the ladder of the needs. Maslow is of the view that gifted have tremendous potential of self-actualisation. That is why they contribute a lot in the progress of the society. Maslow (1968) has suggested how self concept originates and converts into self-actualisation. The development of self-actualisation has been given age-wise which is being presented below:

Infancy Period

Individuals have basic needs that form a hierarchy of growth

1. Basic physical needs (e.g., food and shelter).

Childhood Period

2. Protection, safety and security (physical and psychological)
3. Love, a sense of belongingness (as in a family, a community) and friendship.
4. Respect, esteem, approval, dignity and self-respect.

Adolescence Period

Continuation of growth to higher levels.

Adulthood Period

5. Self-actualisation; the fullest development of one's talents and capacities.
6. Transcendence of self, culture and dichotomies; primarily meta-motivated; behaving and relating to self, others and nature at the very highest and holistic levels of human consciousness.

Source: Barbara Clark: *Growing up gifted* (6th ed.), New Jersey, Merril Prentice Hall, 2002.

Maslow (1968) has suggested certain characteristics found in an individual with self-actualisation. They are described as follows:

- They accept themselves, others and the natural world more.
- Are more authentic, natural and spontaneous.
- Have integrated personality and seek unity.
- Show oneness and increased identification with humanity.
- Are more realistically oriented, aware, more in touch and more perspective.
- Show task commitment, work for a cause, take work like play.
- Appreciate values like truth, justice, beauty etc.
- Like to work for meta-needs.
- Need loneliness for concentrating on any problem.
- Show very high frequency of peak experiences (moments of highest happiness or fulfilment) and frequent mystic, natural or cosmic experiences.

- Are capable of rich emotional reaction and freshness of appreciation.
- Have deep empathy and profound relationship with others; great ability to love and to enjoy sexuality.
- Believe in democratic treatment of others.
- Enjoy life fully. Take challenges happily.
- Have high level of sense of humour.

Source: Barbara Clark: *Growing up gifted* (6th ed.), New Jersey, Merrill Prentice Hall, 2002.

Needless to mention that gifted are self-actualised individuals. But Maslow (1971) feels the need for making some efforts to develop and enhance this characteristic in children. He has suggested certain methods for nurturing self-actualisation among gifted or non-gifted children:

- Listen to your self; trust your inner voice.
- Experience each moment fully, vividly and with total concentration.
- Take responsibility for yourself.
- Think of life as a process of choices, your choices.
- Do what you do with joy, and do it well.
- Dare to be different, non-conforming, real.
- Open up to yourself, identify your defenses and find the courage to give them up.
- Set up conditions that will allow more peak experiences; perceive the world and life positively.

Parents as well as teachers are responsible to provide the facilities at home and school. In fact situation in this regard is very pathetic in our country. The self is the central trait among all the traits of personality. It is a complex and dynamic system of belief that individual holds to be true about himself (Purkey, 1970). In fact self-actualisation depends entirely on the growth of self-esteem which leads the individual toward an integrated personality. Interestingly, sometimes gifted are found with low self concept. The reason may be that gifted set very high expectations from themselves which sometimes may not be possible for them to fulfil. Moreover, parents also have very high level of expectations from their wards. This may lead them toward lower self concept than their age peers. Trotter (1971) has concluded that gifted children often have lower self concepts than average youngsters. Similarly Milgram and Milgram (1976) have confirmed that as gifted children entered adolescence age their self concepts were lowered. This indicates that these children should be tackled in a desirable manner.

Self Esteem

The moment, a child is identified as gifted, the family members start to behave with the child in a different way. The first thinking which comes in their mind is that the child will be able to do without any help in all spheres of life. They set very high expectations from the child keeping in mind that nothing is impossible for that child as he/she is totally perfect. It is quite natural that this affects the child's psychology, especially his/her self-esteem. At that time the child is innocent and ignorant. He goes in an unrealistic world of high self-expectations and tries to maintain the aura of quality. The child begins to consider everything he attempts to be exemplary, over estimates himself and becomes used to being "best" as in the classroom, no doubt, he is able to perform exceptionally.

But excess of everything is bad. When with little efforts, success is expected, it is quite clear that the child may have to face sometimes failure or little success also. This directly affects the child's self-acceptance and esteem adversely developing the feeling of desperation, frustration and anger. However, Hoge and Renzulli (1993) remark that although most intellectually gifted learners have no major deficits in self-esteem but Webb (1994) opines that there are vast numbers of case studies and individual accounts of problems in the area of self-esteem. This may lead them to develop excess of anxiety, worthlessness and other negative characteristics. To reduce or minimise these characteristics parents can play quite a significant role. Clark (2002) has mentioned certain characteristics commonly found in families that produce children with highly actualised potential and self-esteem:

- Parents set clear limits based on each child's ability to understand consequences; goals are clear; success is expected as a right of the child, not of the parent.

- Parental guidance is reasonable, realistic and appropriate to each child.
- The family tends to be liberal and flexible, but not permissive.
- The family is aware of the environment and relates to the environment in a caring, protective way. Children are helped to see their part in the natural order and to respect this unity.
- Parents are relatively self-assured, are on good terms with one another; they accept the responsibility for their own actions.
- Parents lead active lives outside the family and do not rely on their families as the sole or necessarily major sources of gratification and esteem. Vasconcellos (1990) has reported the key findings of The Final Report of the California Task Force to promote Self-Esteem and Personal and Social Responsibility.
- The family is the incubator of self-esteem and the most crucial social unit in a child's life and development. The early months and years of a child's life are the most decisive in establishing a solid base for authentic, abiding self-esteem and depth of personal character.
- The parents' high self-esteem is vital to their ability to provide a healthy environment for the child. We need to extend a great effort to assist parents to develop their own self-esteem and to become more knowledgeable, capable, and effective in nurturing children's positive self-esteem and personal responsibility.
- Because children spend so much of their time in school, the environment of the school also plays a major role in the development of self-esteem. Schools that feature self-esteem as a clearly stated component of their goals, policies, and practices are more successful academically as well as in developing healthy self-esteem.

Moreover, school administration and teachers also are responsible to provide the suitable ambience to gifted students in schools. This is possible when they are made aware of these children's special intellectual needs. They need to know how to organise the classroom for gifted. Besides, gifted should be encouraged to cooperate and accept their peers. Though, it is obvious that specially trained teachers need to be appointed but in-service training courses or orientation courses for teachers cannot be undervalued.

Educational

School Achievement

It is a very well established fact that intellectual ability is positively and highly correlated to the academic performance of children. Hence, gifted too perform highly in the school. Researches have also proved it. Terman et al. (1925) have indicated that gifted students make rapid strides in the field of academics. It is further explained that three out of five of his gifted groups attended kindergarten before entering the elementary grades at an average age of six years and three months. One out of ten in his sample was placed in the second grade on beginning school, and one out of five skipped half of the first grade. By the end of grade school, his group was found to have skipped one entire grade. Terman further says that still the gifted children were found to be below the placement that would be made on the basis of mental age. Witty (1940) has corroborated the views of Terman that these children are far ahead in their studies. The study by Terman *et al.* (1925) also reveals that the measured achievement of the gifted in grade school correlates more highly with intelligence when age was held constant than it did when years of attendance in school were used. In another investigation, Terman and Oden (1947) have indicated that the gifted are more often winners in essay contests and of class honours in elementary and high school. It is clear from the study that they obtain more scholarships to college than do the less adept, and once in college they contribute a disproportionately higher number of members to honour rolls and honorary organisations. A higher percentage of the gifted group pursues work at the graduate level in college than is characteristic of the average college graduate. The investigation conducted by Miles (1954) reveals that if the average gifted child were promoted to his mental age, he would be at least 2.8 years advanced by the age of seven and five or more years accelerated by the age of eleven.

There has been a controversy regarding the assessment of achievement of gifted education, *i.e.*, whether the achievement should be assessed by the grades assigned to their school work or achievement tests. The confusion was removed by Witty (1940) by saying that the results tend to be the same. Barnett, (1957) concluded that the teachers rate these children as superior in the areas like reading, grammar, arithmetic, literature, science, composition, history and geography. They excel to a lesser degree in areas which are not correlated so highly with intelligence, such as penmanship, shopwork, art and sewing. The gifted tend to receive a larger proportion of As and Bs than do the students of average intelligence. This seems to hold true even when the children have been accelerated and are competing for grades with older classmates. These views have been supported by Shannon (1957). Cohler (1941) and Johnson (1942) have found correlation between achievement and intelligence, higher for moderately superior children than for highly superior children.

Gallagher (1985) opines that contrary to popular opinion, which pictures gifted students as constantly bored with and antagonistic toward school, most gifted children like school and love to learn. Hallahan and Kauffman (1991) support Gallagher's view. They say that many gifted students are younger than their classmates because of their superior academic performance. It has also been concluded that gifted girls may complete a four-year college degree by the age at which most students finish high school. Although only the most highly gifted are so far advanced beyond their age-mates, some gifted students start school earlier or advance through the grades more quickly than their age peers.

Gifted Underachievers

Some of the gifted children exhibit unexpected behaviour including performance in school subjects. They show the discrepancy between their intellectual level and school achievement. The school achievement is far below than the expected achievement. Children with these characteristics are categorised as gifted underachievers. These children have been recognised as a unique subgroup within the population of gifted (Callahan, 1981). Pippart and Archer (1963) attempted to identify gifted underachievers in schools and found that there exist discrepancies between achievement test scores and intelligence test scores or between academic grades and IQ.

These children show unhappiness, dissatisfaction, bored, disappointment and are frustrated in their school as well as home life. The reasons behind this are many, like lack of interest in studies, unsuitable or irrelevant curriculum which is unable to satisfy their mental hunger, undesirable study habits, lack of motivation and unsuitable teaching strategies and so on. As a result, these children may involve themselves in anti-social activities as they have to utilise their surplus abilities and capabilities somewhere whether it is desirable or undesirable. They can become top class criminals also.

Researches have revealed that underachievement is affected by the personality of students (Anderson, 1961; Miller, 1961; Delisle 1982; Whitmore, 1980 and Whitmore, 1986). Shaw and Grubb (1958) concluded that a personality trait "hostility" was characteristic of bright underachieving students in comparison with bright achieving students. Barnett (1957) from an intensive study of 32 gifted children chosen on the basis of intelligence test scores over 130 on the Henmon-Nelson Advanced Test, found that the underachievers exhibited a negative attitude toward school. In his study, children with weak performance in the elementary school did even more poorly in the secondary school. Gallagher (1979) observes that children characterised by underachievement have low self-concept, unable to persevere, lack a sense of purpose, feel inferior and experience family conflicts. However, Gallagher has highlighted the problems which one can face while trying to know the cause and effect relationship between underachievement and other negative characteristics of gifted children.

It is worth mentioning that underachievement and non-productivity are different terms. Delisle (1981) has clearly stated that underachievement must not be confused with non-productivity. One should not expect from a gifted child constant productivity in any field. Unfortunately, these children are not cared for in a desirable fashion. Crow (1978), Rimm (1986) and Kos (1993) have observed that teachers, counsellors and administrators look too shallowly for underlying factors while ascribing too readily mental, physical or emotional handicaps to underachievers. Delisle (1982) and whitmore (1980) remark that a very frequent cause is an inappropriate school programme—school work that is unchallenging and boring because the gifted student has already mastered most of the material. They also opine that gifted underachievers often develop negative attitude toward school. Very obvious it is that when a child shows negative attitude, his/her special talents or abilities are surely likely to be overlooked. Gowan (1960) summarised the findings of a dozen research studies in an effort to formulate a comprehensive picture of various factors contributing to underachievement or fostering achievement. He reported nineteen factors accounting for achievement and eight for underachievement, most of which were either personality or environmental factors. Gifted underachievers have been described as disorganized, unmotivated, lacking interest in school, having poor study skills and lacking in self confidence (Rimm, 1986). Krugman (1960) remarks that in the Talent Preservation Project of New York City which was concerned with gifted underachievers, almost 5000 9th and 10th grade students, out of 50,000 in 39 schools scored in the 90th percentile or higher on the Iowa Test of Educational Development and registered an IQ of 130 or higher (The IQ score was obtained from the group test of intelligence regularly administered in each of the participating schools. The schools were permitted to use one of several group tests, such as the Henmon-Nelson and Lorge-Thorndike, which are appropriate for the 9th and 10th grade level). Of these it was found that considerably more than half were not achieving at an arbitrarily agreed upon standard and thus might not have been chosen by teachers as gifted students. Smith and Luckasson (1992) remark that some of these children are hyperactive, while others are passive. Some are bored with school; others are frustrated by the experience. Clearly these students need a strong motivation to succeed. These youngsters need specialised educational services to teach them how to achieve in school, how to approach learning tasks more meaningfully and how to use their talents to the maximum level.

Underachievement of gifted and talented children can result from any of the factors that lead to underachievement in any group such as emotional conflicts or poor home environment (Hallahan and Kauffman, 1991). ASCD (1988), Sizer (1992) and Orlosky and Smith (1978) on the basis of their investigations, reached the conclusion that in the vast majority of schools, the emphases are on knowledge and behaviour. These children in fact do not find the school ambience suitable as well as interesting to their mental level as it does not meet their mental needs. This results in carelessness in school activities. According to Crow (1978) and Plucker and Mc Intir (1995), the gifted child shows poor behaviour by absences, undone homework, wandering attention or "normal" acting out. This unusual and unexpected behaviour is taken in a very different form as the cause of the particular type of behaviour is unknown. The teachers and parents think that the child is ignoring and rejecting them, the authorities of the school and knowledge as well (Tempest, 1974).

Due to this ignorance, the child receives an undesirable treatment. Punishment is considered as the most suitable measure to mend these children's negative behaviour. Holt (1969) and Plucker and McIntir (1995) have proved that punishment includes behavioural restrictions, potentially placement in special classes, grade retention and suspension or expulsion from the school. Apart from this Whitmore and Maker (1980) have found that they are awarded low grades, diminished and negative expectations in the form of punishment. But Supplee (1990) does not agree with the treatment of punishment as it decreases the self-regard of these children. The reality is that this negative behaviour from teachers and parents takes the child to make him stubborn and indifferent as Seeley (1993) and Delisle (1994) have proved that punishment helps exacerbating an already threatening situation. Peabody (1991) and Kos (1993) also support this view and remark that these children are also likely to develop distrust of the system that has treated them inappropriately. Shaine observes that society, at best, gets less of a contribution than it might; at worst, a very bright criminal may emerge. The cost either way, is incalculable, but very large both to the individual and to society. The investigator further suggests that we need to identify the potential hidden behind the problems of these bright and unhappy youngsters and help our students to recognise and develop their abilities. Otherwise, as Kos (1993) has remarked these children develop low self-esteem, while either under-utilising or misapplying their abilities. Supple (1990) has highlighted the characteristics of teachers who teach gifted underachievers. It has been stated that effective teachers of underachievers frequently spend more time unteaching learned negative attitudes and behaviours than teaching academic subjects. On the other hand Whitmore and Maker (1985) opine that the issues of these children vary as one would expect.

It is very important to mention the name of Whitmore (1986)

whose view is that lack of motivation to excel is usually the result of a mismatch between the student's motivational characteristics and opportunities provided in the classroom. Students are typically highly motivated when:

(*a*) The social climate of the classroom is nurturant.
(*b*) The curriculum content is relevant to the student's personal interests and is challenging.
(*c*) The instructional process is appropriate to the student's natural learning style.

Whitmore has also suggested an approach to the problem of underachievement that is consistent with gifted students' advanced reasoning abilities:

- The teacher should study the problem systematically by observing the student's performance and behaviour in various settings.
- The teacher should share those observations with the student, indicating the hypothesised causes of the problem.
- The teacher should attempt to develop a sense of partnership between the student and the parents or teacher(s) involved in the problem.

Belcastro (1985) has expressed that behaviour modification techniques may enhance certain desirable attributes of gifted students-their ability to analyse situations and devise means of coping with hostile or boring environments. However, Gallagher (1979) and Ralph, Goldberg and Passow (1966) have reached the conclusion that counselling and a shift to a more demanding or a more permissive environment have not produced notable success.

The most important step to avoid underachievement among gifted is early intervention. Clark (1979) in this regard has very rightly remarked that the younger the child is when intervention occurs, the more likely the success. Shaine suggests that it is left to us to learn to hear the announcement made by these children through their behaviour about underlying causes of their solution.

4

Identification

Criteria

Identifying children with giftedness is the first step when we go for implementing the educational programmes for these children. We have to be very careful during identification process. Abeel, Callahan, and Hunsaker (1994) have reviewed the literature related to identification process. They have suggested some important aspects which play a vital role in this process:

(*i*) For identification purposes the term giftedness needs to be taken in broad sense.
(*ii*) Many criteria should be the basis of identification.
(*iii*) Separate tests should be used for measuring different aspects of the personality.
(*iv*) Reliability and validity of the tests used is very important.
(*v*) Appropriate tests for underserved population should be included.
(*vi*) Identification by a single score needs to be avoided.
(*vii*) It should always be based on the needs of the students.

Sanborn (1978) prepared some guidelines for identification procedure of gifted children. Renzulli adapted these guidelines which are being given below:

A. An adequate plan for the identification of gifted and talented individuals requires use of a variety of techniques over a long period of time.

(*a*) There are many ways in which the gifted and talented may express themselves.
(*b*) Gifted talented performances may emerge at certain times in life and under certain opportune conditions.

B. Identification of gifted and talented individuals should be based on knowledge of the individual, the cultural-experiential context in which the individual has developed, and the fields of activity in which he performs.
(*a*) At least some methods of identification should be individualised, yielding case study data unlikely to be obtained by group standardised methods.
(*b*) Identification techniques can be locally developed, with methods and criteria which are appropriate for the particular population to be studied.
(*c*) The identification process should call for systematic involvement of those professionals who are acquainted with individuals through direct observation of behaviour and performances.
(*d*) The identification process should call for involvement of those persons best qualified to judge the quality of a performance or product. This is especially important in areas such as the visual and performing arts.
(*e*) The identification process should involve persons best qualified to understand the culture and specific circumstances of individuals whose performances are being assessed.

C. Both self-chosen and required performances should be assessed.

D. Considerable freedom of expression of response should be allowed.

E. Adequacy of the identification programme should be continuously re-assessed.
(*a*) Follow up study should involve both those who were identified as gifted and talented and those who were not.
(*b*) On the basis of evidence obtained, methods and procedures for identification should be modified by refining, adding and deleting.
(*c*) On the basis of evidence, those individuals who have been misclassified may be reclassified as appropriate.
(*d*) Evidence obtained during the identification process school should provide a primary basis for programming experiences and opportunities.

Renzulli and Delcourt (1986) have suggested that identification should be done on the basis of following four criteria.

- Test scores
- Academic mastery in specific domains such as mathematics.

- Creative productivity in specific domains or interdisciplinary areas, with products being assessed by teacher judgement and student interest and willingness to pursue advanced follow-up activities.
- Long-range creative productivity (the ultimate criterion, which can be used to identify gifted persons only after knowing their performance).

Giftedness is not only one factor rather many other factors are included in it. Therefore, it cannot be measured and identified only using one or two factors tests. A combination of different types of techniques are suggested to be used for the identification purposes.

Teachers' Judgement

To ask teachers about children's specialities is the most commonly used technique. The teachers' role in the educational life of a child is of immense value. They can easily notice that in which areas the child is ahead and performs extraordinarily. Among the supporters of teachers' judgement technique the name of Gear (1976) is important who commented that screening programmes for gifted students rely heavily on teachers' refferal. Due to this significance, teachers' ratings have been widely used in selecting the gifted and their educational placement as well. Marland (1972) has proved the wide use of teachers' ratings or nominations for identifying gifted children. The following table makes it clear.

Major Procedures Used and Recommended in the Identification of Gifted Students

Ï.No.	*M jor Identific tion Procedures*	*Per cent Using nd Î nk Order*	*Per cent Î ecommen-ding (nd Î nk Order)*	*Î nk Order Difference*
1.	Teacher observation and Nomination	93 (1)	75 (3)	–2
2.	Group School Achievement Test Scores	87 (2.5)	74 (4.5)	–2
3.	Group Intelligence Test Scores	87 (2.5)	65 (6)	–3.5
4.	Previously Demonstrated Accomplishment (including school grades)	56 (4)	78 (2)	+ 2
5.	Individual Intelligence Test Scores	23 (5)	90 (1)	+ 4
6.	Scores on Tests of Creativity	14 (6)	74 (4.5)	+ 1.5

Gear (1975) observes that studies of teacher nomination often rely on group intelligence tests which are of questionable reliability in the case of extreme scores. Martinson and Lessinger (1960) corroborate this view. Pegnato and Birch (1959) have reported that teachers were not good at identifying gifted students in their classrooms. The investigators had previously identified the gifted students (who had IQs of 136 or above). After that they applied seven criteria including teacher judgement. The researchers found that teachers referred only 45 per cent of those identified as gifted. It was also noted that approximately 31 per cent of those identified by the teachers had average IQs. The researchers have presented their findings which are given below:

Effectiveness and Efficiency of Screening Procedures

Ïcreening Methods	*Number Ïelected by Ïcreening Method*	*Number Identified s Gifted by Ït nford-Binet*	*Effectiveness**	*Efficiency ***
Teacher judgement	154	41	45.1	26.6
Honour roll	371	67	73.6	18.0
Creativity	137	14	15.5	10.2
Art ability	66	6	6.6	9.1
Music ability	71	8	9.9	11.2
Student council	82	13	14.3	15.8
Mathematics achievement	179	50	56.0	27.9
Group IQ Test cut-offs				
IQ 115	450	84	92.3	18.7
IQ 120	240	65	71.4	27.1
IQ 125	105	40	43.9	38.1
IQ 130	36	20	21.9	55.5
Group achievement test	335	72	79.2	21.5

* Per cent of gifted located, N = 91.

** Ratio of number selected by screening to number identified as gifted, in per cent.

Source: Pegnato, C.W. and Birch, J.W.: *Locating Gifted Children in Junior High Schools; A Comparison of Methods.* Exceptional Children, 25, 1959.

The study by Pegnato and Birch is not away from criticism. Critics have pointed out that:

1. Giftedness was based only on IQ; it was possible that the teachers might have used some other factors also for identification purposes.
2. Teachers were not aware of the definition of the term giftedness. So they applied their own perception of giftedness.

But Gear (1978) is hopeful in this regard by remarking that if teachers are trained, they can identify gifted more correctly. So Gear trained a group of teachers regarding the definitions, their characteristics and criteria used to determine giftedness. The results of the study indicated that the trained teachers correctly identified approximately 86 per cent whereas the untrained correctly identified only about 40 per cent. The results revealed very clearly that the training helped the teachers removing the ambiguity about the nature of the term giftedness.

Moreover, Baldwin (1962), Cornish (1968), Jacobs (1971) and Pohl, (1970) also are not satisfied with the teachers' nomination technique for identifying gifted children. Besides, Walton (1961) has remarked that on many occasions teachers were restricted in the number of students they could nominate, thus limiting the possible effectiveness of nomination. Researchers have tried to study the difficulties with teachers due to which they sometimes do not identify correctly. Howley, Howley and Pendarvis (1986) have concluded that the more mixed the ethnic and racial composition of the class, the more difficult it was for a teacher to identify giftedness. Coleman (1985) also attempted to know the difficulties with teachers. It was found that teachers had more difficulty identifying younger students than older, secondary level students. Pegnato and Birch (1959) are also in favour of some guidelines or training to teachers. They said, "In all probability, if teachers were given instruction .... teacher's selections of potentially mentally gifted children would be an effective screening method."

Rating Scales

Some professionals of the field are in favour of applying structured instruments to minimize the problems raised by teachers' nominations. Among those instruments perhaps the most important and widely used is the scale constructed by Renzulli *et al.* (1976). This scale measures four major areas:

(*i*) Learning characteristics
(*ii*) Motivational characteristics
(*iii*) Creativity characteristics
(*iv*) Leadership characteristics

All these areas have 8, 9, 10 and 10 items respectively. Thus 37 items in total. The scale is used by teachers who give their opinion about the child on all the abovementioned items. Examples are like this:

- The child has quick mastery and recall of factual information (measures learning ability).
- The child needs little external motivation to follow through in work that initially excites him (measures motivational characteristics).
- The child is sensitive to beauty, attends to aesthetic characteristics of things (measures creativity characteristics).
- The child participates in most social activities connected to school, can be counted on to be there if required (measures leadership ability).

The child is rated on five points, *i.e.*:

- Almost all of the time
- Never
- Seldom
- To a considerable degree
- Occasionally

But the scale suffers from some shortcomings also such as Renzulli *et al.* could not make clear what they mean by 'to a considerable degree' as well as 'occasionally.' Therefore, teachers while rating the child, are confused. Moreover, the scoring pattern does not speak about the cut-off point to make clear who are the children with superior abilities. Taylor and Sternberg (1989) write that Renzulli *et al.* recommend that users do not total the scores but rather interpret the scores from the major areas separately depending on the 'type of programme' for which a student is being considered.

Borland (1978) also has constructed the scale for identifying children with superior abilities. Fliegler (1961), De Haan (1964) and Gallagher (1966) are the supporters of structured instruments for identifying gifted students. Their views are corroborated by Kirk (1966) who concluded that teachers are more accurate in assessing a child's overall mental ability if they evaluate separate, specific abilities and then form a composite than if they try to give a gross estimate only.

Rating scales undoubtedly can identify really gifted students if constructed in a desirable fashion. But unfortunately many of these scales have certain limitations like improper construction and some are simply lists of behaviours with little criteria established as to how many a student must demonstrate to be considered gifted (Taylor and Sternberg, 1989).

The most important characteristics of any measuring instrument are reliability and validity. But the fact is that many of these rating scales suffer from lack of reliability and validity which lead the teacher or any other rater to subjective judgements. Hagen (1980) has aptly remarked that many were simply a series of ambiguous statements that were checked yes or no and then combined to provide a meaningless score (lack of validity). The subjective nature of many items also leads to disagreement among raters (lack of reliability).

Intelligence Tests

Intelligence is the sole criterion for identifying giftedness in a child. The Stanford-Binet Intelligence Scale published in 1908 is considered the "grandfather" of intelligence tests. This test was used widely over the years till some other tests came into existence like Wechsler Scales. Intelligence tests play the most important role in identification procedure for the gifted children. But despite their significance, these tests suffer from certain limitations. Wilson (1957), Guilford (1967) and Gallagher (1975) have opined that intelligence tests are too limited in scope and higher mental processes such as evaluation, analysis and synthesis are not measured by these tests. Martinson (1973) has highlighted the comparatively small number of items on group intelligence tests and the consequent problem of a "ceiling effect" for gifted children. While Gallagher (1975) has remarked that individual intelligence tests like the Wechsler Intelligence Scale for children (Revised) were the single best indicator of giftedness. On the other hand Matthews (1988) concluded that non-verbal tests such as the Raven's Progressive Matrices are also useful in the identification process of gifted children. However, many researchers, *e.g.,* Renzulli (1971), Bruch (1969, 1973), Torrance (1964, 1969, 1973) and Stallings (1972) have observed the limitations of the use of intelligence tests with the culturally disadvantaged children. In view of the shortcomings of intelligence tests Callahan (1981) opines that the role of intelligence testing as a major variable in selecting students for gifted programmes needs serious revaluation.

Creativity

The latest definition of giftedness includes creativity as one of the important factors. Wallach (1985) observes that "creativity may be best understood as what characterises the work done at the cutting edge of a given field by those who have mastered it." It is also suggested that research should focus on the identification of discipline—specific approaches to improving instruction and the study of creative people's accomplishments as they develop across their entire life spans.

To measure creative potential of any individual is not an easy task. Petrosko (1978) remarks that measuring creativity presents a challenging paradox—devising a standardised way of capturing a non-standard behavioural product. Similarly Treffinger (1986) opines that "we must recognise that creativity is one of the most complex of human functions; it is unrealistic to expect that there ever will be (or that there should be) a single, easily administered, simply scored test booklet that educators can use to decide who is at least one standard deviation above other students in creativity." The importance of creativity has been realised after the Guilford's Model of Intellect who considered creativity as one of the most important factors of intelligence. Obviously this importance pressurised the professionals to construct tests to measure creative potential of individuals. Perhaps very important and widely used test is Torrance Tests of Creative Thinking (Torrance, 1966). There are two forms of this test:

(*a*) Verbal
(*b*) Figural

Both the forms measure four areas, *i.e.,* fluency, flexibility, originality and elaboration. The child is asked the questions related to unusual uses for common objects, improvements in toys, completion of incomplete picture etc. Other important tests which measure creativity dimension are:

- Meeker Structure of Intellect Learning Abilities Tests.
- Guilford's Tests of Divergent Thinking.
- Structure of Intellect Screening Test.

Among Indian tests of creativity are:

- Passi's Test of Creative Thinking.
- Baqer Mehdi's Test of Creative Thinking.

Like intelligence tests, creativity tests have also been criticised on the ground of inadequacy. The real creative potential cannot be measured through these tests as it is affected by many factors. Hocevar's study (1980) revealed that creativity tests do not predict creative behaviour any better than IQ tests do and they are not specific to creative areas such as art or music. Wallach (1970) criticises Torrance's tests and remarks that Torrance Tests seem to be measuring intelligence and do not seem to be measuring creativity any better than intelligence tests do.

Achievement Tests

A specified level of success on a learning task or a certain level of proficiency in any work is called achievement. Educational or academic achievement is a specified level of attainment in academic work as evaluated by teachers, or standardised tests or by a combination of both. Achievement test is a test of maximum performance, *i.e.,* it measures the maximum achievement possible for an individual in an activity. Achievement tests measure the performance of individual after undergoing a course of study. All examinations in schools and colleges make use of achievement tests. These tests are based on the objectives specified in the curricula. They measure the change in behaviour of a child after a period of learning or training. This test is intended to measure the outcome of learning in relation to the objectives of learning the subjects. The child is expected to answer the tests usually within a prescribed time. The total number of correct responses gives an index of child's ability. Achievement tests are either standardised or informal, *i.e.,* made by teacher. These tests are used to measure both cognitive and motor abilities.

For the purpose of identifying gifted children, the use of achievement tests has not been appreciated by some of the professionals. These tests have certain limitations such as they measure the superficial knowledge of the subject. They are unable to measure the thorough and deep understanding of the subject matter. These tests suffer from the ceiling effects as they assess the child average in studies. Martinson (1976), Gallagher (1979) and Renzulli (1978a) have opined that standard achievement tests have serious limitations in their use in identifying or evaluating the gifted child. Callahan (1981) suggests that their usefulness lies primarily in their ability to assess the degree to which the student is able to master the standard curriculum quickly and accurately, and in indicating patterns, strengths and weaknesses in those areas.

Case Study Method

The dictionary says that a case history contains data on family background, social environment, pre-natal and post-natal development, childhood problems, health, physical, social and emotional development, intellectual and personality traits, scholastic progress, peer group relations etc. For educational purposes a case study includes data on family, nature of birth, siblings, early childhood characteristics and problems, health, educational history and psychological characteristics. All items of information considered relevant to the focus of study (purpose) are collected. The methods used for collection of data are interviews with parents, teachers, friends, scrutiny of school records, observation of behaviour and testing. On the basis of the data collected, a precise report is prepared which is called 'case history.' It contains conclusions and recommendations (drawn on the basis of the generalisation from data) which can be used for correctional, remedial or any special treatment suitable for the child. Since a case study is comprehensive, it reveals a lot of information about the child. When a complete understanding of the child is required a case study is undertaken. There are two types of cases studies:

- When complete data on a particular stage of development of the child (*e.g.*, a six year old child) are required 'cross sectional study' is attempted.
- When data on complete development since birth (or for a fairly long period) are required a 'longitudinal study' is undertaken.

Longitudinal studies stretch over many years, while cross-sectional studies are completed within a short period of time. Due to the limitations of other methods of identifying gifted children, case study method has been found more advantageous. If during screening process, the child shows some characteristics of intellectual exceptionality, the information about child's interests, achievements, developments, and other psychological characteristics need to be collected using the format of case studies. Sisk (1988) is in favour of using case study method for identifying gifted children. This method saves economy also. Renzulli and Smith (1977) have reached the conclusion that the case study method is not only an effective method of identifying gifted population rather it is less expensive from economic point of view also. Similarly Renzulli, Reis and Smith (1981) also have proved the advantages of case study method by mentioning that a case study approach, in which aptitude and achievement test scores, teacher ratings, past academic performance, parent ratings and self-ratings are taken into account, has advantages over the more traditional procedures based only on test scores. They further observe that the advantages are greater efficiency and effectiveness in identifying minority group students. In fact all the methods suffer from some shortcomings which is clear by the following table:

Advantages and disadvantages of various screening/identification procedures:

Procedure	*Ïtrength*	*Limit tions*
Teacher judgement (without training)	Inexpensive, time efficient	Accuracy of judgements questionable; possibility of biased decisions.
Teacher judgement (with training)	Predictive accuracy increased over untrained teachers	Time necessary for training is a drawback.
Informal rating scales/checklists	Quick and easy to administer	Lack of reliability and validity.
Renzulli's rating scale	Well researched; relatively well constructed	No cutoffs given; only one section related to IQ.
Individual intelligence and achievement tests	Directly related to identification; scores often used for eligibility	Time consuming
Group intelligence and achievement tests	Time efficient; together predict giftedness fairly well	Good for screening; not for major decision making.
Creativity tests	An attempt to measure an important area associated with gifted students	Difficult area to define and measure.
Tests of specific abilities	An attempt to measure difficult constructs, such as artistic or musical ability	Limited in scope; general lack of information about validity.

Source: Taylor, R.L. and Sternberg, L.: *Exceptional Children: Integrating Research and Teaching*, New York, Springer-Verlag, 1989, p. 222.

The discussion in this chapter reveals that there are various methods of identifying gifted children. We will have to depend on more than one test for identifying the real cases with giftedness.

5

Educating the Gifted

Sometimes it is seen that some gifted lead the life of disadvantaged because desirable attention is not paid to their education only for the reason that they have above average cognitive abilities. This very reality becomes a curse for some of the gifted children as they are considered capable of doing well themselves without providing any extra facilities and arrangements. Researches have revealed that early stimulation at very young age has been fruitful. However, Kauffman and Hallahan (1981) have observed that research on any special population of children and/or special programmes to meet the needs of those children is circumscribed by problems of measurement, questions of ethics of withholding treatment from control groups, statistical analysis, and lack of developmental norms. Further they state that the study of programmes for gifted is fraught with many of these same problems, albeit from a unique perspective.

Terman (1925) and Goertzel and Goertzel (1962) have proved that eminent personalities had enriched experiences in the early years of their lives. Bloom and Sosnaik (1981) remark that parents shared a talent or aptitude with their precocious children and provided role model as well as substantial encouragement as the child began to develop. Pressey (1955) argued that most individuals recognised as outstanding adults were recognised by their families as exceptional at a very young age and given special opportunity. Martinson (1972) remarked that first grade children placed in special programmes for the gifted gained two academic years on achievement measures as compared to the one-year gains of equally gifted children who remained in regular classrooms. On the other hand Sutherland and Goldsmith (1974) have opined that children of superior ability (as indicated by intelligence tests) who are perceived as average by teachers decline in intelligence and achievement relative to equally superior children who are recognised as gifted by their teachers. Getzels and Dillon (1973) favour early identification by stating that bright children placed in first grade early learn more in their first year of school than intellectual peers who remain in Kindergarten.

No doubt that to label a small child as gifted is a difficult task due to the lack of reliability in the measuring instruments. Kauffman and Hallahan (1981) expressed their views that intelligence test scores are notably unreliable for young children, especially when range is restricted. But the ground reality is that though there are many hazards and problems in identifying the children at an early age, its value and utility can never be underestimated and it has been corroborated by researchers like Clark (1979) and Robinson, Roedell and Jackson (1979) also. Nowadays in many families, both the parents are working. In these circumstances, it becomes almost impossible to pay desirable attention to the education of a gifted child. That is why the value of preschool programmes and special educational arrangements becomes more and high. The World Council for Gifted and Talented Children was formed in 1975, to develop a worldwide network and support system of benefit to gifted children and people involved with them. To serve the purpose the council sought the help of international conferences, newsletters, and journals and still it is continuing. This indicates that concerns with and interest in the gifted education is steadily growing worldwide.

Historical Perspective

The history of gifted education tells us about scattered attempts. In ancient period, in Sparta soldiers or people with military skills were respected and given importance to the extent that the skills to fight, show strength in wars, outstanding leadership qualities became the criteria of giftedness. Only upper class boys could receive education in public schools in Athens. Older boys were imparted the education of subjects like mathematics, culture, logic, politics and disputation by experienced and seasoned people. But Plato did not give importance to social status as the criterion of giftedness. He labelled men and women gifted on the basis of intellectual abilities. He was in favour of identifying the most able youths so that they could receive education and show their leadership qualities. In Rome, only men could receive higher education, but doors were opened also for some really gifted women such as Roman matron Cornelia (Good, 1960). Gifted artists, poets, writers, architects were rewarded in Europe, *e.g.*, Leonardo da Vinci, Dante, Michelangelo, Bernini and Boccacio. China also had the idea and provisions of nurturing children with giftedness. According to Tsuin-Chen (1961), at that time China had four principles of contemporary gifted education:

- The Chinese accepted a multiple-talent conception of giftedness, valuing literary ability, leadership, imagination, reading speed, reasoning and other talent.
- They recognized that some precocious youth would grow up to be average; some average youth would later show gifts; and true child prodigies would show gifts and talents throughout their lives.
- They realised that abilities of even the most gifted would not develop fully without special training.
- They believed that education should be available to children of all social classes but that they should be educated according to their abilities.

In Japan during the Tokugawa period, *i.e.,* from 1604-1868, children from poor families were taught only about obedience, loyalty, diligence and submissiveness while Samurai children were taught subjects like calligraphy, history, composition, Confucian classics, martial arts, etiquette, morality and character values.

Developments in America

In the beginning schooling was available to all children, however, some specific arrangements were made for gifted children such as:

- St. Louis in 1870 started the system of passing eight classes in a shorter duration, *i.e.,* less than eight years. Elizabeth of New Jersey in 1886 started a different system in which the gifted child was allowed to complete the studies more rapidly in comparison to other children.

- 'Double Tillage Plan' was started in 1887 by Woburn in Massachusetts. In this system the child was promoted to second semester of second grade only after passing the first semester of first grade. This system was open only for bright children.
- A double track plan was introduced by schools in Cambridge, Massachusetts in 1891. Bright students were taught by special tutors. This system was available only for those students who had the capability of doing accelerated work.
- Following the telescoping grade system, in about 1900, 'rapid progress' classes were started. The gifted child completed the course of three years in two years.
- In 1916, 1919 and 1922 special classes for gifted children were started at different places in America.

Though awareness about gifted education could be seen in America by 1920 but after that (during 1920-1930) fall in awareness was also found due to two reasons:

- During that time emphasis was on imparting education to most of the people. No priority was given to specific education for gifted population.
- Due to Great Depression people were more concerned about their survival only.

Prominent Features

In the beginning, researches were conducted by Sir Farcis Galton (1822-1911) who was the younger cousin to famous Charles Darwin, the author of 'Origin of the Species.' He is known for his contributions in the form of theories about natural selection and the evolution of all species. His contribution is of paramount importance as before that no attention was paid to individual differences among people or issues relating to intelligence and heredity (Clark, 1988). Galton researched intelligence and its measurement. In 1869, he presented his ideas and remarked about some reasons for superior abilities shown by some individuals. He considered intelligence as the keenness of the individuals' senses. He tried to test the intelligence through reaction time, visual and auditory acuity tests and the tests of sensitivity. Galton (1869) wrote the book *Hereditary Genius* devoted to the study of the ability of gifted people. He explained that hereditary factors play an important role in intelligence. After examining the biographies of some eminent personalities, he concluded that "ability, zeal and readiness to work" played a prominent role in their outstanding achievement. He considered the "gift of high ability" as the factor of utmost significance in their high achievement. Moreover, he opined that to become great in a given area one needed a high degree of general ability. Besides, he believed in the great versatility which he found in the early years of future genius. He was of the view that superior abilities are only due to the genetic factors and eminence was due to two factors—first, an internal motivation to excel and, second, the intellect, both of which were thought to be genetically inherited (Callahan, 1981). This conviction still remains.

After that a French Psychologist Alfred Binet (alongwith his colleague T. Simon) was asked to construct some tools to measure the intelligence of those who were unable to get benefit from the general schools as they were not having the normal range of intelligence. They were retarded in their studies and their behaviour too was not normal. They were too quiet, or aggressive or hostile or withdrawn. Binet constructed a number of tests to measure intelligence. Historians of the field like Clark (1988), Gallaghar (1988) and Tannenbaum (1983) emphasise the significance of the deveopment of the Binet's Tests. These tests included the items to judge the memory, attention span, reasoning, comprehension etc. and these factors were matched with the judgements given by the teachers of those dull children. It is Binet who first of all presented the idea that a child may be ahead or behind the intelligence level for his/her chronological age. Hence, Binet is considered the father of 'Mental Age'. He explained that a child's mental and chronological age may be different. In fact Binet's test created the real interest among the people of America about gifted children. Although there were some programmes for the gifted children established as early as 1866, real development and growth in educational services for these individuals did not occur until the 1920s (Maker, 1986). Then comes the name of Henery Goddard who in 1910 (Stanley 1976) successfully identified the intelligence of 400 "feebleminded" children with the Binet-Simon tests, and in 1911, he summarised his evaluation of 2,000 normal children. These tests were evaluated as successful as they could clearly divide the children having average, below average and above average intelligence level.

Lewis M. Terman, a Stanford psychologist studied gifted children in an exhaustive manner. He contributed in the field of gifted education in two significant ways. First he supervised the modification of Binet-Simon tests producing in 1916 the grandfather of all American intelligence tests, the Stanford-Binet Intelligence Scale. The test was revised in 1937, 1960 and 1986 (Colangelo and Davis, 2003). Terman's second gift is in the form of the longitudinal study of gifted children. He identified more than one thousand gifted children and studied them for about more than a half century. Terman authored four volumes of "Genetic Studies of Genius" (Terman, 1925; Terman, Burks and Jensen, 1930; Terman and Oden, 1947 and 1959) which is the most significant study in the field of gifted education till date. He studied these children's educational, psychological, vocational, family life, social and other aspects of life. The results revealed that gifted children were above average in all the studied characteristics. However, Goleman (1980), Sears (1979) and Sears and Barbee (1977) have remarked that those Children were not of the stature of Einstein or Picasso.

Interestingly Stanley (1976) has remarked that Galton was the grandfather of the gifted child movement, Binet the midwife, Terman the father, and Columbia University's Leta Hollingworth the nurturant mother. Her pioneering contributions consisted of personal efforts supporting gifted education and gifted students in the New York City area, from about 1916 until her death in 1939, and the publication of two major books, "Gifted Children: Their Nature and Nurture" in 1926 and "Children above 180 IQ. Stanford-Binet: Origin and Development" in 1942 (Colangelo and Davis, 2003). Very significant difference between Terman and Hollingworth's views regarding the characteristics of gifted children can be seen easily. Terman found these children more emotionally stable while Hollingworth found them as emotionally more unstable to such an extent that they may need counselling. She also suggested that they may need education of emotions which includes how, why, when, where, at what place, to whom and to what extent the emotions should be expressed. This finds support from the quotation by Aristotle who says – "Anyone can become angry-that is easy. But to be angry with the right person, to the right degree, at the right time, for the right purpose and in the right way – this is not easy." No doubt, that Terman's study developed interest in gifted education but there was a gap of efforts by the Great Depression of the 1930 and also World War II in 1939.

The history of gifted education remains incomplete if the launching of the Soviet Satellite Sputnik in 1957 is not discussed. This led some critics to state that Russian science education was better than America's. It was said that America neglected gifted and their education. The launch of Sputnik was taken as a challenge to American education. This provoked the country to catch up and surpass the competition. The government started to think about funding for different programmes' establishment. Efforts were made to identify the students with superior abilities especially in mathematics and science subjects as these students were seen as a great national resource the persons who would make America the leader once again (Smith and Luckasson, 1992).

In 1959, a report *Soviet Commitment to Education* (First Official U.S. Education Mission to the USSR 1959) was published which explained that the typical Russian high school graduate had completed 10 years of math, 5 years of physics, 5 years of biology, 5 years of a foreign language, 4 years of chemistry, and one year of astronomy. The launching of Sputnik was taken as a total talent mobilization (Tennenbaum, 1979). Tennenbaum further observes that academic course work was telescoped for bright students; college courses were offered in high school; and foreign languages were taught in elementary classes. Acceleration and ability grouping were used, efforts were made to identify gifted and talented minority children and new math and science curricula were developed. High schools glittered with new concern for high scholastic standards and career mindedness. Bright students were expected to take tough subjects to fulfil their potentials and submit their developed abilities for service to the nation.

In the development of gifted education, contributions of some reports need to be mentioned. First one is the *Education of the Gifted and Talented* published in 1972. Keeping in view the significant role of the U.S. Commissioner of Education, S.P.

Marland, the report is also called as *Marland Report.* This is the report that brought the gifted education into limelight. The report says that the population of gifted children in America could be 3 to 5 per cent of the whole population. The tragic part was that majority of gifted were not receiving special education, the government did not keep this education on priority which could result in the psychological injuries and harms to this population. The government did not show interest in spending money for the education of gifted. Very prominent impact of the report was the Federal definition of gifted and talented children. According to this definition the criteria of giftedness and talented should be general intellectual ability, divergent or productive thinking or creative potential, ability in performing and visual arts, scholastic aptitude, psychomotor ability and leadership ability. This definition is so comprehensive that even today it is considered as one of the good definitions of giftedness.

Second report entitled *A Nation at Risk* was published in 1983 by the National Commission on Excellence in Education. Though this report did not say much directly about gifted education but it uncovered the neglect of high academic standards and neglect of highly intelligent students.

The third and latest report published in 1993 is *National Excellence: A Case for Developing AmericaÕ Talent.* The report was published by the U.S. Department of Education showing the pathetic condition of America in the field of education. It remarked that America had a "quiet crisis" in educating its talented students. The report has revealed certain issues like America's ambivalence toward intellect, the importance of social/emotional issues, issues of rural schools and urban schools, the challenge of identifying culturally diverse students and the warning of international competition especially in science and mathematics.

Thus the history of gifted education revolves around about 6 eminent scholars, an intelligence test, Sputnik the Russian Satellite and 3 very significant reports published at national level regarding the gifted education.

Acceleration

Efficacy of acceleration is doubtless today. About till 1950 the situation was not very clear in this regard. But with the passage of time, the change in mindset was seen. The National Education Association (1961) has reported, "The research testimony as to the advantages of acceleration is weighty, consistent and continuous over several decades." The dictionary meaning of the word 'accelerate' is to make quicker or to hasten or to increase the speed. In the field of education it is going through an educational programme more rapidly or at a younger age than is usual for the average child (Pressey, 1963). Pressey cites the example also that a child starts school at the age of 6, progresses a grade each year, and so enters the seventh grade at the age of 12. If a child enters at the age of 5 or completes the first 6 grades in 5 years or so to enter the seventh grade at the age of 11, he might be considered a bit accelerated. It is being regarded more favourably than formerly, because ways of accelerating have been developed that are less likely to cause social and emotional maladjustment than grade skipping.

Acceleration is possible through different forms. The student completes the course in a shorter duration of time. He may skip one grade, or half grade or one semester and can be accelerated. According to Clark (2002) acceleration can take many forms, including:

(*i*) Early entrance to formal schooling, which can occur at kindergarten or university level.
(*ii*) Moving through age-graded classes in less time by grade skipping, moving through cross-age grouped or non-graded classes in two rather than three years, or advanced placement.
(*iii*) Moving through curriculum materials and concepts at an accelerated rate by curriculum compacting, telescoping content, or receiving credit by examination.

Clark has explained the forms of acceleration in an exhaustive manner. Many other researchers have also studied it thoroughly and attempted to know how far acceleration is implementable and advantageous to the students as well as the society as a whole. Quite a large number of investigators have shown their choice of acceleration.

Alltucker (1924) studied 135 most accelerated children in the senior high school in Berkeley, California. No child was found to be below average in intelligence quotient and only 80 per cent were average. Over 68 per cent were distinctly above average, ranging in IQ from 115-154. The scholarship was clearly superior among the accelerates 70 per cent were labelled as thoroughly satisfactory or excellent in this respect. The investigator found some interesting results regarding the leadership ability of these children like:

- The percentage of pedagogically accelerated girls who were above average was approximately twice as great as the percentage of pedagogically accelerated boys who were above average.
- The percentage of boys rating below average was approximately the same as the percentage of girls rating above average.
- The ratings for both boys and girls gave a fairly normal curve of distribution.

The study reveals that the teachers reported that from their observations of the selected children, over 70 per cent of the accelerates were liked or admired by their fellow students; that most (70%) were found socially adapted; that over 27 per cent obtained unusual recognition in special appointments (class officers and other appointments). The accelerated child obtained recognition in being selected as a class officer more frequently than the non-accelerated.

Jones's (1912) study is considered as one of the pioneer studies in the field of pedagogical acceleration of gifted. In Massachusetts, children were admitted to the Kindergarten and to the first grade when their mental ages were adequate. Of 258 children, whose chronological ages at admittance were below the average age at which children were usually admitted, 62 per cent were in the upper half of their classes (according to teachers' judgements and marks), and 33 per cent were in the first quarter of their classes, while only 12 per cent were in the lowest quarter of their classes. Of those in the lowest quartile two-thirds had been in school less than 4 months. Educational adjustment of the children was increasingly satisfactory as length of residence in school increased. Of those in school a year or more, only

7½ per cent were in the lowest quarter of their classes. These under-age children had been admitted over a period of 5 years. The findings of the study indicate that under-age children were successful to a degree somewhat above the average for their school grade, and that their ability to excel became more noticeable as they progressed through the grades. However, due to the subjectivity in the study and lack of control group, its results are not considered as reliable.

Freeman (1924) supported the acceleration to the extent that he took it as general educational policy. He laid emphasis on the fact that acceleration as a means of adjustment had advantages not generally accredited to it, that grade skipping as a systematic practice was not as detrimental as had been thought. Freeman remarks:

> Acceleration actually provides enrichment. The work of the advanced grades is intellectually superior because the method which is pursued and the content are superior to those of the lower grades. From the point of view of intellectual adjustment, then acceleration accomplishes both, the saving of time and the enrichment of instructions. The difficulties with this mode of adjustment are not of an intellectual nature but of a social nature. These difficulties may be met by proper forms of organization and they are being progressively eliminated by the very increase in the frequency of acceleration itself.

Sackett (1929) researched on the students who belonged to the Blewett junior high school of St. Louis, Missouri. He compared the success of pupils who had completed a 3 course in 2 years with that of pupils who had spent 3 years in the same junior high school. Both groups were pupils of superior intelligence. It was found that the differences in their scholastic achievements were negligible, although the accelerated group was 8 months younger in chronological age, and 7 points lower in intelligence quotients than the non-accelerated group. The investigator reported also that the accelerates were more likely to be successful in the senior high school if they were selected on the basis of mental, social and physical qualities rather than if they were selected solely because of mental superiority. This group selected for concentrated work during the junior high school did hold its own scholastically in senior high school-even when they were compared with older children of similar IQ. Silverman and Jones (1932) conducted an experiment with 491 students who entered college at 17.5 years of age or younger. The views of these students were collected by the experimenters about things such as difficulties in adjustment to the college situations, scholastic demands and social life. The students were asked whether they would have preferred to enter college later in life, and if so what they would have liked to do with the time saved. In general, those who entered college late thought that others should not enter early. About 7 per cent of the early entrants would have preferred to spend more time in the elementary school. 17 per cent would have been amenable to devoting much more time to high school. About 9 per cent indicated that more time spent in junior college would have been desirable. 67 per cent (remaining) were satisfied with the time allotment given to college preparation. The results of the experiment showed that 7 to 7 per cent felt that because of their age, they were at a disadvantage in social life, in opportunities for leadership, and in athletics. Of older college entrants only 2 to 4 per cent reported this. One third of those who entered college at 17 or younger felt they were at a disadvantage in discussions of social, economic, sociological and philosophical problems, whereas, only one-sixth of older groups reported a consciousness of such a disadvantage. In educational achievement the young students showed no inferiority upon an extensive test; the scores of young students were superior to those of older ones on the college achievement test. Although the experimenters conducted the experiment in an exhaustive manner but it would be worth mentioning at this place that the experiment suffered from certain limitations of the questionnaire used. Nevertheless, it appears to indicate rather clearly that young college students are well adjusted educationally and socially as well.

Dougherty favoured grade skipping on the basis of case studies of 3 accelerated children. It was reported that the academic attainment and general physical and social status of the accelerates were improved after grade skipping had occurred. Moreover, McElwee (1932) studied the elementary school students. Teachers of the second, third and fourth grade were asked to check a miscellany of traits indicating which of the traits described each student in their classes. Groups of 100 accelerated, 100 regularly promoted, and 100 retarded children were selected from the entire enrolment in these grades. There were 50 boys and 50 girls in each group. Equal amounts of acceleration for boys and girls had occurred. A child was designated retarded, if he had been left back one or more terms. The amount of retardation ranged from one to five terms. An accelerated child was one who had been doubly promoted one or more terms. The range was one to three terms. Since 7 of the 14 traits were deemed desirable and 7 undesirable, the researcher assumed that desirable and undesirable adjustment is revealed merely by reference to the frequency with which traits were checked for the children in the three groups. The accelerated children possessed all of the desirable traits to a greater degree, and all the undesirable traits to a smaller degree than did the other group.

In fact acceleration has been researched extensively, and in general the results have come in its favour as Gold (1979) has also remarked. A number of researchers have supported acceleration such as Terman and Oden (1947), Pressey (1955), *Fund for the Advancement of Education* (1957), Bish and Fliegler (1959), Anderson (1960), Reynolds (1962), Lucito (1964), Gallagher (1966), Plowman and Rice (1967), Braga (1969), Alexander and Skinner (1980), Gold (1980) and Morgan, Tennant and gold (1980) etc.

Brady and Benbow (1987) have opined that accelerative strategies offer the student the opportunity to select an educational programme that is challenging, interesting and meets the needs of the individual student. Further they said that this procedure is beneficial to the school because a special curriculum does not have to be developed and implemented. They remarked that for school, acceleration offers "a way to challenge highly able student without the expense and effort of designing a special curriculum."

Hallahan and Kauffiman (1991) although are somewhat doubtful about the efficacy of the acceleration as they have observed that acceleration has not been a very popular plan, except with extremely gifted students. Even then they accept that evidence in favour of acceleration is quite positive. This is proved by the research work conducted by Johnson and Johnson (1987) who are considered the promoters of heterogeneity and cooperative learning. Both the investigators have reported that high-achieving students may need to study material far above their grade level. These students have been suggested by the researchers to be placed in higher grades for certain subject areas during part of the day or having them study advanced material in homogenous groups. Feldhusen, Proctor and Black (1986) prove the advantages of acceleration by summarizing the researches on advanced placement of precocious students. The summary is as follows:

> Examination of the research literature reveals that acceleration contributes to academic achievement. No negative effects on social or emotional development have been identified. If adjustment problems occur, they tend to be minor and temporary in nature. Conversely, failure to advance a precocious child may result in poor study habits, apathy, lack of motivation, and adjustment.

In a study, Gallagher *et al.* (1983) have concluded that acceleration is cost effective also. The results of their study reveal that in 10 states more than $ 19 million in college costs was saved only in one year. Smith and Luckasson (1992), too favour the acceleration as these students are able to handle the academic challenges of acceleration. Second, when grouped with students of comparable abilities, they make greater achievement gains. Third, they develop better self concepts and more positive attitude about course content and school in general. They further opine that this approach is also cost effective, saving parents' millions of dollars in college tuition.

The preceding discussion clearly shows that most of the professionals of the field are in favour of acceleration as it has immense value to the life of a gifted student. This reminds us of the meta-analysis of 26 researches performed by Kulik and Kulik (1984, 1991) to know the effects of acceleration. They reached the results that gifted and talented are able to handle the academic challenge that accelerated programmes provide. They have justified these results with the following report:

First, talented youngsters who were accelerated into higher grades performed as well as the talented, older pupils already in those grades. Second in the subjects in which they were accelerated, talented accelerates showed almost a year's advancement over talented same-age nonaccelerates.

In general, it can be said that there are certain reasons for the favour of acceleration:

(*a*) There is no restriction in the type of school where acceleration is possible.
(*b*) Continuity and coordination needs to be maintained for successful acceleration.
(*c*) Early intervention is always fruitful. If children are accelerated at lower level, they definitely join the college of high standard.
(*d*) Accelerated children help in productivity at an early age.
(*e*) They start to enjoy their career life earlier than non-accelerates.
(*f*) Acceleration avoids development of negative characteristics among gifted as it reduces boredom and negative attitude toward different subjects and school also.
(*g*) Gifted students prefer to be with older friends as they find themselves well adjusted with more matured children.
(*h*) Accelerated children have been found socially, emotionally and personally more adjusted than their non-accelerated counterparts.
(*i*) Class performance of these children is equal or sometimes better than their older classmates.
(*j*) Cost-wise also, acceleration is advantageous. It is cost effective as the child completes his education in lesser time spent in school or college.

It has been mentioned earlier that acceleration can be done in different forms. Fox (1979) has explained in quite detail different forms of acceleration which have been called as Models of Acceleration. The ultimate goal of all the models is one, *i.e.,* the student will complete his/her education in a shorter duration of time. If only one model is implemented, it serves the purpose. All the five major models are being given below:

- *Early admission to schoolÑ* One acceleration technique has been admission of children to kindergarten or first grade one year earlier than usual. This practice is not widespread despite a number of studies which indicate its positive benefits for gifted youngsters.

- *Early admission to college or admission with advanced standingÑ* This alternation for gifted students occurs at the other end of the public school grade structure and is far more common. Fox says that contrary to belief, many colleges are willing to accept students who do not have high school diplomas. While Solano and George (1976) have reported that many gifted students are ready for college as young as fourteen years of age.
- *Grade SkippingÑ* Due to fear of maladjustment and lack of information, this practice is employed less now than fifty years ago (Solano and George, 1976).
- *Telescoped ProgrammesÑ* It is called as telescoping grades also. Fox has the opinion that in this technique student's programme is telescoped, *i.e.,* 3 years are condensed into 2 years, or 4 years into 3 years. This practice is most common in ungraded elementary schools and junior high schools. Like grade skipping, it presumes that the child is generally gifted, *i.e.,* across subject matter areas. Fox further states that second method of telescoping (more commonly used by high schools) is to allow students to complete high school graduation requirements in a shorter period of time by eliminating or reducing courses, earning credit by examination, skipping courses, taking summer courses, and/or carrying extra courses.
- *Subject matter accelerationÑ* The philosophy behind this model of acceleration is that the student may not be outstanding in all the subjects or courses. Therefore, the student can skip or telescope only a particular subject or course on the basis of achievement in the class. Clark (2002) opines that although acceleration should not be used as the total plan for a gifted programme, the literature shows very few disadvantages to this provision when used on individual basis. No doubt, acceleration has many advantages for the child as well as society but we have to be very careful about its implementation, *i.e.,* only most deserving students (extremely gifted) should be given this opportunity. Otherwise, chances may be there that the fears related to acceleration will come before us in the shapes of disorganised

society.

Opponents of this programme put an alarm to the society about the problems which the student and ultimately the society has to face. Coleman (1985) has expressed the fear that acceleration might lead to social or emotional maladjustment as it frequently results in the teaching of the same material, only teaching it faster. However, Birch, Tisdall, Barney, and Marks (1965) and Whitmore (1981) do not agree with the findings of Coleman (1985). Southern, Jones and Fiscus (1989) do not support acceleration due to the social and emotional maladjustment that these children can develop when they are grouped with older children. This type of placement may be harmful for accelerated gifted and they may become scornful of their age peers. Renzulli (1978) is sceptical about acceleration programmes' overall success. The argument is that these programmes may help gifted in achieving high performance in the field of academics but not in professional productivity rather they may restrict the child's potential for such productivity.

The discussion in the preceding pages clarifies that majority of the professionals of the field encourage acceleration programmes for the students who really deserve it. Very few are there who do not favour this programme. However, Kauffman and Hallahan (1981) observe that attempts have not been made to compare the achievement or characteristics of similarly gifted students who do not elect such programmes or who drop out of them.

The Enrichment Triad Model

Renzulli was not satisfied with accelerating the gifted students as it fails to meet the mental demands of the child in school. The logic behind this is that in acceleration the student does not get any extra curriculum and other activities to study and do. But when the child is provided with the enrichment programme, definitely he/she gets something different from the regular curriculum which successfully meets the educational needs and thus the potentials of the child can be easily harnessed. Renzulli has emphasised more on creative productivity of the gifted. Therefore, to do justice with gifted in this regard he suggested an Enrichment Triad Model originally in the mid-

1970s to encourage and boost up the gifted potential. The triad is as below:

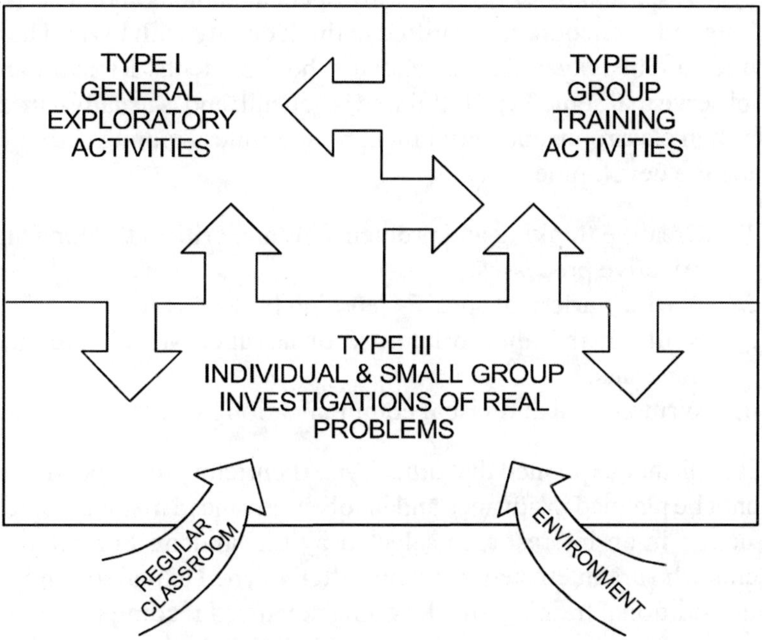

Source: http://sp.uconn.edu/~nrcgt/sem/semexcl.html accessed on 2/20/04.

The diagram of the enrichment triad model depicts that there are three types of enrichment. Renzulli & Reis have remarked that the enrichment triad model has been designed to encourage creative productivity on the part of young pupils by exposing them to various topics, areas of interest, and fields of study and to further train them to advanced content, process-training skills and methodology training to self selected areas of interest. The triad consists of three types of enrichments given below:

Type I Enrichment Programmes—This enrichment programme consists of a team of parents, teachers and students. The team plans to expose students to various topics, disciplines, events, places, hobbies, persons and occupations which are not included in regular school programmes. The team arranges mini-courses, demonstrations of performances, speakers to make the students learn about the subject matters or topics which are of high difficulty level. This task can be done also by distributing films, slides, videotapes or other print or non-print materials. The regular class students are also encouraged to participate in these activities.

Type II Enrichment ProgrammesÑ Special methods and materials are designed to encourage the gifted to think deeply with logic. These activities are also available to regular school students. Renzulli and Reis observe that some Type II training is general, and is usually carried out both in classroom and enrichment programme. Training activities include the development of:

1. Creative thinking and problem solving, critical thinking and affective processes.
2. A wide variety of specific learning how-to-learn.
3. Skills in the appropriate use of advanced-level reference materials.
4. Written, oral and visual communication skills.

It is further explained that other Type II enrichment is specific, as it cannot be planned in advance and involves advanced methodological instruction in an interest area selected by the student. For example students who are interested in botany, after a Type I experience might pursue additional training area by doing advanced reading in botany; compiling, planning and carrying out plant experiments and seeking more advanced methods training if they want to go further.

Type III Enrichment ProgrammesÑ It is for the students who are interested in pursuing a self-selected area and are willing to commit the time necessary for advanced content acquisition and process training in which they assume the role of a first hand inquirer. The goals of this programme are:

- Providing opportunities for applying interests, knowledge, creative ideas and task commitment, self-selected problem or area of study.
- Acquiring advanced level understanding of the knowledge (content) and methodology are used within particular disciplines, artistic areas of expression and interdisciplinary studies.
- Developing authentic products that are primarily directed

toward bringing about a desired impact upon a specified audience.
- Developing self-directed learning skills in the areas of planning, organisation, resource utilisation, time management, decision making and self-evaluation.
- Developing task commitment, self-confidence and feeling of creative accomplishment.

The Enrichment Triad Model serves directly to 15 to 20 per cent population of the school. Renzulli and Reis (1986) have stated that this model seeks to modify the entire educational system. The model offers a different view of education for all children by allowing students to move into advanced level activities on the basis of their performance in general enrichment offerings. Renzulli has emphasised on three components most while defining giftedness:

- Above average ability
- Creativity
- Task commitment

The Enrichment Triad Model has been appreciated by a large number of school authorities and other concerned persons. But the question is how does this programme work. Smith and Luckasson (1992) explain that students "revolve" into and out of different level programmes. Another question may be that for attending these programmes, the student will have to devote some extra time in school. But the situation is that some minutes from other subjects' teaching are curtailed and during that time the student has to perform activities. This is called Curriculum Compacting.

The Revolving Door Identification Model

This model is based on the notion that children exhibit gifted behaviour in relation to particular projects or activities on which they bring to bear their above average ability, creativity and task commitment (Hallahan and Kauffman, 1991). Delisle and Renzulli (1982) state that this model has received widespread attention. Torrance (1962, 1974) concluded on the basis of a research study that students who were rated highly creative do well in school and on achievement tests but are often not selected for gifted programmes as their scores are often below the cut off for admission. Renzulli, Reis, and Smith (1981) demonstrated that in Revolving Door Identification Model (RDIM) a talented student receives regular enrichment experiences and the opportunity to 'revolve into' Type three creative productive experiences. These researchers have recommended that in RDIM, the students be selected for participation in the talent pool on the basis of multiple criteria that include indices of creativity because of the belief that one of the major purposes of gifted education is to develop creative thinking and creative productivity in schools. Renzulli and others remarked that once identified and placed in the talent pool through the use of test scores, teacher, parent or self-nomination and example of creative potential or productivity, students are observed in classrooms enrichment experiences for signs of advanced interests, creativity or task commitment. Kirschenbaum (1983) and Kirschenbaum and Siegle (1993) have demonstrated that students who are rated or test high on measures of creativity tend to do well in school and on measures of achievement.

The experiences of Enrichment Triad and RDIM gave birth to a new work by Renzulli and Reis (1985, 1997) that is called: *The Schoolwide Enrichment Model (SEM).*

Based on enrichment triad model, the schoolwide enrichment model considers schools the places for talent development. The school provides opportunities which are challenging and enjoyable to gifted. Renzulli and Reis proposed the model and presented the Executive Summary of the same. Hard work by the two researchers in the form of detailed field testings and exhaustive researches for about 20 long years helped them to propose the model. They explain that the SEM shows the impact of three principal bodies of research:

- It is designed around the body of research evidence indicating that instruction must take into account the varying abilities, background interests, experiences and learning styles of each student.
- Learning is more meaningful and enjoyable when content and process are learned within the context of a real problem and when students use authentic methods to address the problem.
- The model builds on research suggesting that all students

including low income students need to be provided with challenging and accelerated learning content. Learning experiences are therefore, designed with the goal to engage and offer stimulation and enjoyment to all students.

The most important purpose of this model is to address the need to reduce the "separateness" of special and regular programmes and to make certain that students who can profit from enrichment activities are given opportunities to engage in more challenging activities (Hallahan and Kauffman, 1991). But the goals of "curriculum compacting" as Starko (1986) observes are to create a challenging learning environment, guarantee proficiency in basic curriculum and make time for enrichment and acceleration.

Major Components of the Schoolwide Enrichment Model

Curriculum Compacting

Modifying or 'streamlining' the regular curriculum in order to eliminate repetition of previously mastered material, upgrade the challenge level of the regular curriculum, and provide time for appropriate enrichment and/or acceleration activities while ensuring mastery of basic skills.

Assessment of Student Strengths

A systematic procedure for gathering and recording information about student's abilities, interests and learning styles.

Type I Enrichment: General Explanatory Experiences

Experiences and activities that are designed to expose students to a wide variety of disciplines (fields of study), visual and performing arts, topics, issues, occupations, hobbies, persons, places, and events that are ordinarily covered in the regular curriculum.

Type II Enrichment: Group Training Activities

Instructional methods and materials that are purposefully designed to promote the development of thinking and feeling processes.

Type III Enrichment: Individual and Small Group Investigations of Real Problems

Investigative activities and artistic productions in which the learner assumes the role of a first hand inquirer: the student thinking, feeling and acting like a practicing professional.

Source: F.R. Olenchak and J.S. Renzulli, The effectiveness of the schoolwide enrichment model on selected aspects of elementary school change. *Gifted Education Quarterly*, 33 (1), 1989.

In fact the SEM is not rigid so far as its implementation is concerned. Schools have the freedom to make changes according to the convenience, peculiarities of the gifted population, available resources, interests of students etc. It helps improving the entire school ambience. It serves as a practical plan for K-12 teachers and administrators. The model consists of three basic elements:

The Total Talent Portfolio

Students complete various instruments and contribute their best work samples to reflect their strengths and interests as learners. Documenting their abilities, interests and learning style preferences allows for appropriate decision making in all curricular areas. This information focuses on students' strengths rather than deficits, and is used by schools to decide which talent development opportunities to offer particular students.

Curriculum Modification Techniques

The model encourages the development of a challenging curriculum, and one that injects both in-depth and enrichment learning experiences into regular school activities. Curriculum modification may be necessary, and can be done through textbook analysis, curriculum compacting (elimination of repetitive or previously mastered material, improvement of the challenge level of the regular curriculum, and provision of time for enrichment and acceleration activities), and an expansion of the depth of learning (a focus on representative topics and ideas, and an emphasis on students' roles as firsthand investigators).

Enrichment Learning and Teaching

The development of the school programme should be based upon the following four principles of enrichment learning and teaching:

- Each learner is unique
- Learning is more effective when students enjoy what they are doing.
- Learning is more meaningful and enjoyable when content and process are learned within the context of a real and present problem.
- Some formal instruction may be used, but a major goal is to enhance knowledge and thinking skills acquisition through inductive teaching and the application of knowledge and skills that result from student's construction of meaning.

Source: http://www.ed.gov/pubs/ToolsforSchools/sem.html accessed on 12/24/04.

The abovementioned elements can operate within three types of school structures which are being given below:

- *Regular Curriculum*
  The most important purpose of the SEM is not to replace rather enhance the regular curriculum. This enhancement is possible only through integration of curriculum modification and differentiation and all the Type I, Type II, and Type III of Enrichment Triad Model.
- *Enrichment Clusters*
  These clusters means multi-age groups of students who meet regularly with a facilitator to share and pursue a common interest. Clusters which revolve around major disciplines, interdisciplinary themes, or cross-disciplinary topics, emphasise the development of higher-order thinking skills and the creative and productive application of these skills to real-world situations.
- *Continuum of Special Services*
  Supplementary services including individual or small group counselling, mentor relationships and direct assistance in facilitating advanced level work are essential for a talent development programme to be effective in meeting the needs of individual students.

The model improves the school structure including all the factors which affect the learning process. The implementation of the model needs money also which differs from school to school. Some extra arrangements like salary, material for a part-time Enrichment Specialist, one full time specialist are needed in the schools where students' number is more.

To know whether the schoolwide enrichment model is successful, researches have been conducted that suggest the model has been implemented in the schools having students from different socio-economic status and ethnic background. It has also been implemented in various educational settings. The results of the implementation have been found positive. The researches in the field of Schoolwide Enrichment Model can be divided into various categories such as:

(*a*) The effectiveness of the model as perceived by key groups.
(*b*) Research related to creative productivity.
(*c*) Research relating to personal and social development.
(*d*) The use of the model with underserved populations.
(*e*) Research on self efficacy.
(*f*) The use of the Schoolwide Enrichment Model as a curricular framework.
(*g*) Research relating to learning styles and curriculum compacting.
(*h*) Longitudinal research on the model.

The review of literature reveals that some other curriculum models have also been developed by professionals. These models are being presented below:

Product Development Model

Stephens (1996) developed this model which has a process of seven-steps:

- First step encourages the students to select a topic for investigation.
- Second step is for students create a list of questions to answer.
- Step three tells the students to establish a time line.
- Students select a media to convey the knowledge obtained,

in the fourth step. Computer programmes, advertisements, drawings, maps, photos, experiments, plays, speeches may be some of the samples of media.

- Fifth step is for students' presentation or displaying the project to an audience.
- Sixth step calls for students to celebrate in a stress-free informal environment and share what was learned.
- Seventh and last step provokes the students to reflect on the process and perform a self-evaluation.

Autonomous Learner Model

This model is developed by George Betts to help gifted students develop skills of independent learning (Northwest Regional Educational Laboratory, 2000). The model has five stages.

- *The orientation stageÑ* The students develop an understanding of their abilities, interests and learning styles.
- *Enrichment activities stageÑ* The students explore content and interests.
- *Seminar stageÑ* Groups of students work together with others who have similar interests.
- *Individual development stageÑ* Students develop skills for problem solving.
- *In-depth study stageÑ* Students pursue their individual interests.

Feldhusen and Kolloff's Three-Stage Model

Feldhusen and Kolloff (1978) emphasised more on independent learning activities in the curriculum designed for gifted students. They developed a model for enrichment activities. The model is for gifted having the IQ range between 110-140. However, they are in favour of acceleration for the students with higher than 140 Intelligence Quotient. This model has three stages:

Stage One

In stage one the development of convergent and divergent thinking abilities are considered most important. Feldhusen and Kolloff emphasise on the development of certain skills like fluency, flexibility, originality, elaboration, analysis, evaluation etc.

Stage Two

After completing stage one the child should go for second stage where he has to solve more complicated problems and do the activities that need creative problem solving ability. Simulation games need to be emphasised to achieve the objective. Covington, Crutchfield, Davies and Olton (1966) have recommended the use of the Productive Thinking Programmes as they help the child to utilize fully the cognitive abilities.

Stage Three

In this last stage the gifted is suggested to work on projects independently. The child should be given the liberty to choose the project from the area of his/her own interest. The procedure of completing the work should be:

- Identification of the problem
- Collection of data from books and other resources.
- Interpretation of the data.
- Communication of the data creatively.

Feldhusen and Kolloff have given some important guidelines:

- Standardised achievement tests as well as teachers' observations should be used for identification of gifted, creative and talented children.
- Identified students should be organised into small groups that meet at least twice a week for guidance and enrichment activities.
- Formulation of instructional objectives and their use as guides in planning all activities should be given due importance.
- Intellectual stimulation and challenge should be considered important which are possible through activities.

- Children should be encouraged to study independently.
- Much stress should be there on challenging reading and discussion.

Thus, in the end it can be said that acceleration and enriched curriculum are not suitable to all the gifted students. It depends on the individual student what educational programme is suitable to him/her. Teachers have to be very careful whether the child should be accelerated or provided with the enriched curriculum.

6

Indian Scenario

The condition of education of gifted or talented in India is far from satisfactory, rather pathetic. However, some efforts have been made which are being discussed below.

National Talent Search Scheme

NCERT started a scheme in 1963 to identify the talented students of India, under the name of the National Talent Search Scheme. In the beginning the scheme was started as a pilot project. Only 10 scholarships were provided to the students of class XI belonging to the Union Territory of Delhi. But only after a year, *i.e.,* in 1964 the number of scholarships was increased to 350 and the scheme was extended to the whole country. The scheme was only for science students with 55 per cent marks in class X and studying in class XI under the 11 year schooling pattern. In the states where the pattern was different, the students studying in the equivalent class were considered eligible for applying for the scholarship. The applicants had to appear in the examination which consisted of a Science Aptitude Test, an Essay Paper, a Project Report and if selected then interview. Till 1965 scholarships were granted only up to graduation. But a change was made in the scholarship scheme in 1966. It was extended up to Ph.D. degree. A significant aspect of the scheme was that there was a provision of nurturance of talent. To serve the purpose summer schools were organised to update the knowledge of the students at undergraduate level in their respective fields. In addition to this, the students studying in post graduate classes were provided the facility of placement programmes.

In 1970, the Science Aptitude Test Papers were printed in 15 languages recognised under the Constitution of India. This action was taken to reduce the language bias in the examination. The students had the freedom to write an essay and prepare a project report in the language of their own choice. Besides, during this very time Agricultural Sciences were included within the scope of Basic Sciences. After that students belonging to agricultural sciences were also eligible for applying for the award of scholarship.

The executive committee of the NCERT appointed a Review Committee to look into the functioning of the scheme and suggest changes if necessary. The committee suggested some modifications which were implemented in 1977. The scheme was extended to Social Sciences, Engineering and Medicine also. In order to reduce the subjectivity in the assessment, the essay paper and the project report were removed. The scheme was made open to the candidates of X, XI and XII classes. The examination for all these classes were conducted separately. The number of scholarships was raised to 500. Some changes in the selection procedure were also made. There were two tests. Mental Ability Test (MAT) and Scholastic Aptitude Test (SAT) followed by interview. The composite marks of all the three tests were the basis of result. In 1981 the number of scholarships were raised from 500 to 550. These extra 50 scholarships were reserved for the students belonging to SC/ST category. But again it was thought to make some changes in the number of scholarships and in 1983 the number was enhanced to 750 (70 scholarships for SC/ST students). The number of scholarships distributed amongst the awardees of class X, XI and XII was 375, 150 and 225 respectively. This centralised scheme of NTSE continued till it was decentralised in 1984 and implemented in 1985.

The decision of the implementation of decentralised pattern of the scheme was taken in a meeting held in Delhi on 12-13 April 1983. The meeting was attended by the liaison officers of all the States and Union Territories. In the new decentralised scheme only the students preparing for X class examination were eligible. Thus all the stipulated 750 scholarships were awarded to the class X students. Sharma (1988) after analysing the decentralised pattern of the scheme expressed his views about its genesis which are as follows:

- Identification of talent at later stage is not desirable as the students at higher class show the effect of achievement and it appears more like a merit scholarship than a talent search one.

- The new decentralised pattern aims at covering a wider catchment area to explore talent in the far flung areas of villages, as it is visualised that at the state level, at least three to four times more centres will be opened.
- The class X examination, by and large, is a public examination all over the country and consists of almost all common compulsory subjects of study.
- Since the scheme was in operation for classes X, XI and XII, in some of the states where there was 10+2 pattern, the candidates were getting two chances, while in some other States (with the 11 year schooling pattern) candidates were getting only one chance to appear in the talent search examination. This inequality of opportunity is obviated in this pattern.
- The involvement of state authorities was considered desirable as they had a feeling that they were not directly involved in such an important project. The new pattern provides for a participative strategy of selection in which first level screening is to be done by each State.
- The organisation of three examinations (class X, XI and XII) in fifteen languages for over one lakh candidates spread over more than 440 centres all over the country was, no doubt, a tedious managerial exercise. The new pattern lessens the burden of management tasks and aims at focussing more attention on academic exercises for improving evaluation procedures of selection of candidates for the award of scholarships.

Further Sharma (1988) has presented the salient features of the decentralised scheme:

- *Limited to class X*—The scheme was applicable only to class X candidates. All the 750 scholarships from 1985 onwards were to be awarded to class X candidates. The candidates studying in class X of any type of recognised school were eligible to appear at the state level examination from the state in which the school was located.
- *Two stage testing*—The decentralised system provides for a two-stage testing and screening of the candidates. The first

stage screening was undertaken independently by the respective State/Union Territory. Each State/Union Territory would sponsor the names of the successful candidates (for which a quota was fixed) to the NCERT. The second stage testing was to be undertaken by the Council. This examination was an open competition for all these candidates. The final selection of the candidates for the award of scholarships was based on their performance in the written examination followed by the interview.

- *Quota system*—In order to allow the candidates to compete for the second stage testing, a quota was fixed for each and every State/Union Territory. The number of candidates to be admitted for the national level examination from a State/Union Territory was proportionate to the enrolment at the secondary stage, subject to a minimum of 25 in the case of a state and 10 in the case of a Union Territory with maximum of 500 from any State/Union Territory.
- *Linkages with parental income*—Unlike the previous system, the award of the scholarship was now linked with the income of the parents of the awardees. The awardees whose parental income was less than Rs. 1000/- per month would receive the scholarship at full rate. However, candidates whose parental income was more than Rs. 1000/- per month would receive half the rate of the scholarship.
- *Separate administration of the MAT and SAT*—Under the new pattern, the MAT and SAT were administered separately. Earlier it was a composite test consisting of Part-I and Part-II, administered together as one test paper.
- *Minimum qualifying marks*—Unlike the previous system, the new system provided for minimum qualifying marks in each part of the test. A candidate from the general category had to secure a minimum of 40 per cent marks in MAT and also 40 per cent marks in SAT in order to qualify for the written examination. However, a 20 per cent rebate was given to the scheduled caste and scheduled tribes.

The details of MAT and SAT are like this – The MAT which consisted of 100 multiple choice type of questions was to be attempted by all the candidates. The SAT consisted of 25 multiple choice type questions each on 8 subject areas namely mathematics, physics, chemistry, biology, history, geography, civics and economics. The students could choose any 4 out of these 8 subjects and had to answer a total of 100 questions in the SAT.

Again in 1995 a vital change in the scheme was made. Now the candidate had no choice in the SAT, *i.e.,* all the subjects were made compulsory. They were science (40 questions), social science (40 questions) and mathematics (20 questions). In addition to this the number of scholarships was enhanced from 750 to 1000 in the year 2000. There was a provision of reservation for schedule caste and schedule tribe candidates based on the national norms of 15 per cent and 7½ per cent respectively.

Procedure of selection consists of two stages. First stage selection is conducted by the individual State/Union Territory while the second stage selection is conducted by the NCERT.

First stage selectionÑ The examination is conducted by each State/ UTs which have the autonomy regarding the norms for the purpose of determining the eligibility of the candidates. Only after passing this examination, the candidates are allowed to appear in the second stage examination. The students' merit list is prepared for the eligibility to second stage selection.

The students belonging to class X of Navodaya Vidyalayas, Kendriya Vidyalayas, Sainik schools and others are eligible to appear in the examination. The medium of examination is announced by the State/UTs.

Second stage selection—After qualifying the first stage test the candidate may appear in this examination. This test is open for all the students of Indian nationality whether they are studying in India or abroad. The standard of the questions is of class X level but there is no prescribed syllabus. The candidates have to appear in both the tests, *i.e.,* MAT and SAT which are administered separately with a short interval in between.

The MAT consists of 100 multiple choice type items with five alternatives, out of which only one answer is correct. Each question carries one mark. The candidates are provided with the answer sheets separately for answering the items.

The SAT too consists of 100 multiple choice items with four alternatives. Each item carries one mark. There is no negative marking.

The items belong to the science, social science and mathematics subjects. The medium of the test is English or Regional languages recognised under the constitution of India. The examination is conducted by the Centre Superintendent.

Candidates selected on the basis of merit are called for interview. Interviews are arranged at different places all over the country depending upon the number of candidates found eligible from different regions. The award of scholarship is declared on the basis of both National level written examination and the interview. There is no provision of re-evaluation of scripts.

The candidates from Basic and Social Sciences including commerce are awarded the scholarship up to doctoral level. But the students studying in professional courses such as medicine, engineering, management and technology are awarded the scholarship up to second degree level. The awardees can attend the Nurturance Programmes for their own benefit arranged by the NCERT.

National Talent Promotion Scheme

The NTSS awards 1000 scholarship to regular students every year and there is another scheme for dropout students. The purpose of the scheme is to bring these students into main stream. The NCERT has planned to start the scheme from the session 2005-2006 and 100 students from across the country will be offered the scholarship. In identifying dropout students help from national and state open schools will be sought. Dr. V.K. Jain, head of the Committee on the scheme explains that "the objective is to find students who are inclined towards education and are trying hard to complete their schooling despite the hardships. The target is not students who prefer to sit at home than studying."

The scheme is open for students who are at the end of their elementary schooling stage or rather who are in class VII or VIII. The selected students can be helped to complete their postgraduate courses and Ph.D. in sciences and social sciences.

Jawahar Navodaya Vidyalayas

One of the important suggestions of the New Education Policy 1986 was the establishment of Navodaya Vidyalayas in rural parts of the country to educate the rural talented children. The aim of these schools was to provide opportunities chiefly to the children of rural areas so that they could learn how to live together, how to learn together and thus develop their potential. To serve the purpose, the government of India constituted the Navodaya Vidyalaya Samiti to govern these schools. NVS is an autonomous body which functions under the Ministry of Human Resource Development.

These schools were started in 1986 all over the country except Tamil Nadu. The first Jawahar Navodaya Vidyalaya was started at Navsari, Amravati. These schools are residential, co-educational, fully financed by the government of India. Children are educated free of cost, *i.e.,* free board and lodging, stationary, uniform, medical care etc. However, a nominal fee of Rs. 200 per month is charged from the students belonging to IX to XII classes. But girls and the children coming from the families whose income is below poverty line and SC/ST have not to pay the fees. The district magistrate is the ex-officio chairman of these Vidyalayas where education is provided from VI to XII classes.

Objectives

The objectives are to:

- provide high quality modern education.
- inculcate values.
- involve the students in adventurous activities.
- provide physical education.
- introduce them to the components of culture.
- make the students aware of the environment.
- give the knowledge of their culture.
- develop the feeling of national integration through migration system.
- promote their talents and capabilities in different areas.
- provide in each district, focal points for improvement in the quality of school education in general.
- make the students competent in three languages (as visualised in Three Language Formula).
- establish the pace setter institutions as models in the districts and as resource centres for excellence promotion.

The education in these schools is imparted regardless of socio-economic status of children.

Selection Procedure

Students are selected for admission on the basis of a test designed and also conducted by Central Board of Secondary Education (CBSE). The nature of the test differs from other admission tests as it is a non- verbal test and class neutral. Moreover, it is so designed as to ensure that talented children from rural areas are able to compete without facing any disadvantage. The number of students to be admitted each year is 80 but due to the lack of physical facilities, only 40 students are admitted annually. The school administration tries to admit at least 75 per cent students from rural areas and out of this one third are girls. The syllabi are prepared by the NCERT. The medium of instruction is mother tongue or regional language upto class VIII and English thereafter for mathematics and science and Hindi for social sciences. The syllabi include three language formula: the third language taught is either the regional language (other than Hindi) or in Hindi speaking area, the language of that proportion of the schools' student population coming from another region on the annual exchange programme, who spend a year at the school. This block of students constitutes 30 per cent of the annual intake. The emphasis is on continuous comprehensive evaluation, keeping in mind the cognitive, affective and psychomotor domains for the all round development of the Child. Since evaluation is very important aspect of teaching process, teachers as well as principals of the schools are imparted special training in this regard.

Another significant feature of the syllabi is the *Migration: An experiment in national integration*. It is a scheme of exchange of students. 30 per cent students of a particular linguistic region from a Navodaya Vidyalaya are migrated to another Vidyalaya in a different linguistic region. The purpose is to promote understanding of the diversity and plurality of India's culture and people. The interesting part of this scheme is that migration takes place between Hindi and Non-Hindi speaking districts. Migration depends on students' voluntary willingness or they are selected by lottery (if sufficient number of students is not available). The District Magistrate selects the students for migration. Due attention is paid during the migration of students from the remotest part of the country between Vidyalayas located in east, west, north and south India. It is also seen whether migrated students are well adjusted in other Vidyalayas. But most of the time they are found very well adjusted.

Cocurricular Activities

These activities are one of the important features of these Vidyalayas. National Sports Meets are organised by Vidyalayas to identify talented students in sports. The purpose of this type of meets is to develop physical and neuro-muscular skills, fitness, sportsmanship and spirits of cooperation. Different types of sports are encouraged in some of the vidyalayas located in tribal areas of the country like gymnastics, archery and judo etc. Navodaya students are imparted NCC training and they attend camps also and have proved their potentials in the area. These students also participate regularly and actively in the Scouting and Guiding. It will not be out of place to mention that NVS is recognised as a State for Scouting and Guiding activities by the Bharat Scouts and Guides. Besides, students get the opportunities of debating, art, elocution and other activities.

Navodaya Vidyalays organise a number of activities with other institutions, schools, groups in the local community such as:

- Participation of students in local community centres and social services.
- Provision and sharing of audio-visual facilities.
- Interaction of teaching staff with the teaching staff of neighbourhood schools.
- Promotion of library facilities for the community and introduction of Mobile Library Schemes.
- Adult literacy classes.
- Use of service of school staff nurses for promoting health and hygiene in local community.
- Participation of local teachers in workshops and seminars.

Most of the pass outs of these schools have succeeded in seeking admissions in different professional courses like medical sciences, engineering, information technology etc. The average pass percentage is more than 80 per cent which is significantly higher than the overall success rate of CBSE schools.

Navodaya Leadership Institutes

The Navodaya Vidyalaya Samiti organises training facilities for teachers to equip them with latest knowledge in their own and other fields also. The main purpose of the training is to provide quality education. Five training centres have been established informally by the NVS within the available infrastructure in the Vidyalayas campuses at Ghaziabad, Guntur, Hyderabad, Goa and Chandigarh. Teachers from across the country come to these centres to receive in-service training and for refresher courses as well.

Aims of Training

- Identification of the needs of the teachers and organisation of different types of inservice courses.
- Encouragement and coordination of innovative practices, experiments, action researches and survey projects etc.
- Development of curriculum enrichment material for in service courses.
- Evaluation of the practices and procedures of the school system and suggestion for further improvement.
- Development of effective low cost teaching aids and acquainting teachers with the latest educational technology. The Samiti organises the following types of courses:
  (*i*) Short-term refresher courses for subject teachers on content analysis, testing, innovations and evaluation for a duration of approximately 6 days to one week.
  (*ii*) Content oriented in-service training courses for PGTs and TGTs in different subjects for a duration of 2 to 3 weeks depending on the nature of the course.
  (*iii*) Pre-service training induction courses for the Principals, PGT or TGT. The duration is 21 days.
  (*iv*) Capsule courses of 3 days duration on specific subject areas such as remediation, setting up question papers, evaluation etc. depending upon the requirement of teachers.

During the training programme lecture method is used as minimum as possible. Other methods like case study, group work, discussion, role play, problem solving, field visits, project work and investigation are used to the maximum level. More emphasis is laid on some factors. They are:

- Implementation of National curricular plan.
- Importance to new teaching strategies.
- Safety and security of stakeholders.
- Use of different audio-visual aids.
- Inculcation of moral and value oriented education.
- Identifying training needs, prioritising, planning, implementation and evaluation of the training programme.
- Use of electronic media devices.
- Increasing competitiveness in work.
- Creation of congenial residential culture.
- Remedial teaching.
- Continuous comprehensive evaluation.
- Looking to pool up the talents of professionals with a concern to work in teams.
- Proper interpersonal human relationship.
- Timely completion of specific works of staff.
- Effective communication.
- Full attendance of stakeholders.
- Promoting excellence.
- Responding the accountability.
- Minimizing disruptive tendencies of productivity.

Apart from this, much emphasis is on interaction and participatory approach in teaching and learning process, educational technology, value orientation, appropriate interpersonal human relationship and the right kind of environment in the schools. Continuous pre-service and in service training of teachers are arranged by the NVS in collaboration with NCERT, RIE, NIEPA etc.

The coverage of Navodaya Vidyalayas is quite high in the districts which are educationally backward. In some of the States like, Manipur, Jammu & Kashmir, Karnataka, Dadara & Nagar Haveli etc. 100 per cent coverage has been made.

Statewise Details of JNVs Sanctioned/Uncovered Districts and their Percentage as on 15th October, 2001

Sl. No.	*Name of State/UT*	*Total No. of Districts*	*JNVs Sanctioned*	*Balance Districts*	*Percentage Coverage*
(1)	(2)	(3)	(4)	(5)	(6)
1.	Andaman & Nicobar	2	2	0	100
2.	Andhra Pradesh	23	22	1	96
3.	Arunachal Pradesh	15	12	3	80
4.	Assam	23	20	3	87
5.	Bihar	38	37	1	97
6.	Chandigarh	1	1	0	100
7.	Chhatishgarh	16	11	5	69
8.	Dadra & Nagar Haveli	1	1	0	100
9.	Daman & Diu	2	2	0	100
10.	Delhi	9	2	7	22
11.	Goa	2	2	0	100
12.	Gujarat	25	19	6	76
13.	Haryana	19	18+1	1	95
14.	Himachal Pradesh	12	12	0	100
15.	Jammu &Kashmir	14	14	0	100
16.	Jharkhand	22	21	1	95
17.	Karnataka	27	27	0	100
18.	Kerala	14	13	1	93
19.	Lakshdweep	1	1	0	100
20.	Madhya Pradesh	48	45	3	94
21.	Maharashtra	35	31	4	89
22.	Manipur	9	9	0	100
23.	Meghalaya	7	7	0	100
24.	Mizoram	8	6	2	75
25.	Nagaland	8	6	2	75
26.	Orissa	30	24	6	80
27.	Pondicherry	4	4	0	100
28.	Punjab	17	17	0	100
29.	Rajasthan	32	32	0	100
30.	Sikkim	4	3	1	75
31.	Tamil Nadu	30	0	0	0
32.	Tripura	4	4	0	100
33.	Uttar Pradesh	70	66+1	4	94
34.	Uttaranchal	13	12	1	92
35.	West Bengal	19	6	13	32
	Total	604	509+2	65	89

Source: navodaya.nic.in/jnvs.htm accessed on 28/6/05.

The Government of India has labeled these schools as especially meant for rural talented children. No doubt, sufficient space is given to cocurricular activities in these schools. In fact gifted or talented education needs the enriched curriculum while the students in Navodaya Vidyalayas have to study the curriculum designed by the NCERT which is not fully enriched curriculum, and is not suitable to talented children.

Parenting

Parents are the first teachers of every child. To be a parent of a gifted child is quite challenging and demanding. It is necessary for parents to have the knowledge of characteristics of gifted children. It helps them to know parenting techniques. Usually it is seen that parents of gifted children lack the knowledge of how to deal with their intellectually superior child. The cognitive superiority sometimes may prove as a curse for the gifted.

It is most important for parents to know the difference between a bright child and a gifted child. The bright child is the one who always seems to have the answers to the teacher's questions. A gifted child is the one who questions the answers. They are divergent thinkers or to put it more plainly they are just a little bit different from the rest of the general population. And being different is never easy. Most of the parents think and expect too much from a gifted child. They do not know the educational services to be provided to their child as well as their role as parents. Hackney (1981) and Colengelo and Dettmann (1983) have proved through their researches that many parents of academically talented children are confused about their role with the schools and uncertain about how to advocate appropriate educational services for their gifted children. Since the child has surplus abilities, he is expected to do the best in all the areas without any guidance or help from others. This is the point which takes the parents toward wrong doings. No doubt, some gifted are more verbal and exhibit exceptional abstract thinking skills and they seem to be more mature than other children of their age (Davis and Rimm, 1989). But these unusual characteristics help deceiving parents. It is surprising to know that some of the parents do not like to accept the child's giftedness as they want to think and show that the child is completely normal and well adjusted while some other parents accept the child's giftedness and pressurise the child to achieve and excel in all areas.

In fact, in every child's growth, the role of family and home can never be underestimated. Clark (2002) has commented – "The home is in my mind, the true cradle of eminence. Whatever we find in our world that we would like to change, we must begin with parenting if we are to have a lasting impact". To love and to be loved, is a psychological urge. This urge can be satisfied only in the family and parents are responsible for its satisfaction. Researches have revealed the specific characteristics of the family of gifted children. Important researches have been conducted by Baumrind (1989), Bloom (1982), Cornell and Grossberg (1987), Davis and Rimm (1994), Karnes, Shwedel and Steinberg (1984), Olszewski, Kulieke and Buescher (1987), Rimm and Lowe (1988) and Satir (1972). These characteristics are summarised below:

- Gifted come from small families having few children.
- The gifted may be the only child or the first child in the family.
- Family provides enrichment activities to the child such as taking him to exhibitions, museums, art galleries, encouragement to language development, providing reading materials etc.
- Parents believe in strong work ethics.
- They are highly educated and love to learn.
- They are also energetic like their children.
- They have authoritative parenting styles.
- Parent-child relationship is healthy and interaction among all family members is desirable.
- Children receive respect and dignity from their parents.
- Parents develop the feeling of independence in the child for doing all the activities.
- Works, learning and play are shared by parents also.
- Children get the opportunity of early stimulation.

Source: B. Clark, *Growing up gifted* (6th ed.,) Merrill Prentice Hall, New Jersey, 2002.

Role of Parents

Parents are supposed to play the most prominent role in the life of their gifted children. Some important points in this regard are like this:

A gifted child is always in search of answers. Parents should be the providers of answers. The child should be provided challenging experiences. He should be given the opportunity of discussing all types of topics. Parents need to encourage the child to read many books. They should motivate the child to develop research skills. Moreover, they themselves should develop the love for reading creatively and critically too. The child should be allowed to think and work independently. He should be given the liberty to consult atlases, encyclopaedias, maps etc. Parents should listen patiently whatever the child explains. They should not hesitate seeking help in dealing with a gifted child from the experts of the field. They are expected to provide complicated problems to the child as this will boost up his problem solving ability. The child needs to be appreciated for his unusual ideas, questions, imaginations etc. as this helps developing the ability of invention. Parents are expected to show their child's unique works among their friends' circle. This lets the child feel recognised by others. The child needs to be encouraged to find out the answer himself first.

Gifted are more sensitive, possessive, compassionate and touchy. Parents have to be more conscious about the emotions of the child which directly affect the social behaviour. Ann Marie Roper in her article *The Emotional Needs of Gifted Children* has remarked – "Gifted Children overflow with emotion, passion, enthusiasm. At times they exhaust others with their emotionality." Parents are required to exhibit the behaviour that does not develop in children negative psychology, *i.e.,* feeling of inferiority, frustration, depression and mental stress. They need to play a role model on certain important issues like punctuality, discipline, honesty and other moral values. Although the child needs extra attention to satisfy his mental demands but excess of extra attention should always be avoided as this may lead the child to develop a weak psychology.

Parents are expected to keep themselves concerned with school issues. Surveys have confirmed it. Alsop's (1997) survey of forty two parents of young children (with mean age of 6.9 years) who scored above IQ 130 (mean =150) on the Stanford Binet L-M revealed that 61.7 per cent expected their child to have a special teacher and 51.1 per cent expected special classes, yet the most common opportunity the schools actually offered to their children was extensions of learning in the normal classroom. Feldhusen and Kroll's (1985) survey of 385 parents whose children attended a Saturday enrichment programme offered by a University revealed that 42 per cent of parents of preschoolers, 47 per cent of parents of children in grades 1-6 and 53 per cent of parents of youth in grades 7-12 felt their children's needs were not being met in schools. Moon *et al.* (1997) are also of the view that parents of gifted children are highly concerned with the school activities of their children. Frequent meetings with school authorities are necessary for desirable development of the child. Parents need to be careful about the educational choices of the child. Besides, whatever the child has done before the schooling was started, should be brought to the knowledge of the teachers. This helps knowing the fields of interests of the child. They need not to hesitate if they want to give some suggestions to meet the child's educational needs. They can form 'parents' association of gifted children.'

It is clear from the above discussion that giftedness is not a challenge for children only, rather it creates challenging situations for parents too. All the parents need to take care of themselves as well as their children. This helps them build stronger self-esteem and better parenting abilities.

Bibliography

Abeel, L., Callahan, C. and Hunsaker, S. (1994). The use of published instruments in the identification of gifted students. Washington, DC: National Association for Gifted Children.

Abraham, W. (1958). *Common Sense about Gifted Children.* New York: Harper & Row.

Alexander, P. and Skinner, M. (1980). The effects of early entrance on subsequent social and academic development: A follow-up study. *Journal for the Education of the Gifted*, 3(3), 147-150.

Alltucker, M.M. (1924). Is the pedagogically accelerated child a misfit in school? *School Review*, Vol. XXXII, March, pp. 193-202.

Alsop, G. (1997). Coping or Counselling: Families of intellectually gifted children. *Roeper Review*, 20(1), 28-34.

Amabile, T.M. (1989). Growing up creative, New York Crown.

Anastasi, A. and Levee, R.F. (1959). Intellectual defect and musical talent: a case report. *American Journal of Mental Deficiency*, 64, 695-703.

Anderson, K. (Ed.) (1960). Research on the academically talented student. Washington, DC: National Education Association.

Anderson, K.E. (Ed.) (1961). Research on the academically talented student. Washington, DC.: National Education Association.

Anderson, M.A., Tollefson, N.A. and Gilbert, E.C. (1985). Giftedness and reading: A cross sectional view of differences in reading attitudes and behaviour. *Gifted Child Quarterly*, 29(4), 86-189.

Armstrong, M.E. (1955). A comparison of the interests and social adjustments of underachievers and normal achievers at the secondary school level. Doctoral dissertation, (Stross, Connecticut: University of Connecticut). Abstract in Dissertation Abstracts, 15, 1349-1350.

Association for Supervision and Curriculum Development (1988). *Content of the curriculum.* Alexandria, VA: Association for Supervision and Curriculum Development.

Ayres, L.P. (1956). Money cost of repetition versus the money saving through acceleration. Division of Education, Russell Sage Foundation, Bulletin No. 111.

Baker, H.J. (1949). Characteristics of superior learners and the relatives merits of enrichment and acceleration for them *Supplementary Educational Monograph*, 69, Chicago: University of Chicago Press, October, pp. 153-154.

Baldwin, J.W. (1962). The relationship between Teacher-judged giftedness, a group intelligence test, and Kindergarten pupils. *Gifted Child Quarterly*, 6, 153-156.

Ballard, P.B. (1922). Group tests of intelligence. New York, Hadder and Stoughton.

Barbe, W. (1954). *Differentiated guidance for the gifted. Education*, 74, 306-311.

Barbe, W.B. (1956). A study of the family background of the gifted. *Journal of Educational Psychology*, 46, 302-309.

Barbe, W.B. (1957). What happens to graduates of special classes for the gifted? *Educational Research Bulletin*, 36, 13-16.

Barnett, H.O. (1957). An intensive study of 32 gifted children. *Personnel Guidance Journal*, 36, 192-194.

Barnett, L.A. and Fiscella, J. (1985). A child by any other name .... A comparison of the playfulness of gifted and non-gifted children. *Gifted Child Quarterly*, 29(2), 61-66.

Barnett, W.L. (1957). Advance credit for the superior high-school student. *Journal of Higher Education*, 28, 15-20.

Bauer, A.M. (2000). Terman's studies of the gifted. In Encyclopedia of special Education, Second Edition, Vol. 3, Edited by Reynolds, C.R. and Elaine Fletcher-Janzen, John Wiley and Sons, New York, pp. 1781-1782.

Baumrind, D. (1989). Rearing competent children. In W. Damon (Ed.), *Child Development Today and Tomorrow* (pp. 349-378). San Francisco: Jossey-Bass.

Belcastro, F.P. (1985). Gifted students and behaviour modification. *Behaviour Modification*, 9, 155-164.

Bentley, J. (1937). Superior children, New York, W.W. Norton Co., p. 67.

Binet, A. and Henri, V. (1896). La psychologie individuelle. *Annee. Psychol.*, 2, 411-465.

Binet, A. (1909). Les idees modernes sur les enfants. Paris, Flammarion.

Birch, J., Tisdall, W., Barney, D. and Marks, C. (1965). A field demonstration of the effectiveness and feasibility of early admission to school for mentally advanced children. Pittsburgh: University of Pittsburgh.

Bish, C. and Fliegler, L. (1959). Summary of research on the academically talented student. *Review of Educational Research*, 39, 408-450.

Bloom, B. (1982). The role of gifts and makers in the development of talent. *Exceptional Children*, 48(6), 510-522.

Bloom, B.S. and Sosnaik, L.A. (1981). Talent development vs. schooling. *Educational Leadership*, 39, 86-94.

Boehm, L. (1962). The development of conscience: A comparison of American Children of different mental and socioeconomic levels. *Child Development*, 33, 575-590.

Bond, H.M. (1957). The productivity of national merit scholars by occupational class. *School and Society*, 85, 267-268.

Bonsall, M. and Stefflre, B. (1955). The temperament of gifted children. *California Journal of Educational Research*, 6, 195-199.

Boring, *E.G.* (1923). Intelligence as they tests it. *New Republic*, 34, 35-37.

Borland, J. (1978). Teacher identification of the gifted. *Journal for the Education of the Gifted*, 2, 22-31.

Braga, J.L. (1969). Analysis and evaluation of early admission to school for mentally advanced children. *Journal of Educational Research*, 63, 103-106.

Brody, L. and Benbow, C. (1987). Accelerative strategies: How effective are they for the gifted? *Gifted Child Quarterly*, 31, 105-109.

Brown, W. and Yakimowski, M. (1987). Intelligence scores of gifted students on the WISC-R. *Gifted Child Quarterly*, 31, 130-134.

Bruch, C. (1969). A proposed rationale for the identification and development of the gifted disadvantaged. *Unpublished manuscript*. Athens, Ga.: Department of Educational Psychology.

Buffington, P. (1987). Perfection: Impossible dream? *Sky*, 16(8), 31-34.

Burks, B.S., Jensen, D.W. and Terman, L.M. (1930). The promise of youth: follow up studies of a thousand gifted children. Genetic studies of genius, Vol. 3, Stanford, Ca.: Stanford University Press.

Burt, C. (1955). The evidence for the concept of intelligence. *British Journal of Educational Psychology*, 25, 158-177.

Burt, C. (1962). The gifted child. In B. Bereday and P. Lauwerys (Eds.) *The Yearbook of Education*, New York: Harcourt Brace Jovanovich.

Callahan, C.M. (1981). Superior abilities. In J.M. Kauffman and D.P. Hallahan (Eds.), *Handbook of Special Education* (pp. 48-86). Englewood Cliffs, NJ: Prentice-Hall.

Carrol, H. (1940). *Genius in the Making*. New York: McGraw-Hill Book Co., Inc., pp. 115-121.

Cassel, R. and Haddox, G. (1959). Comparative study of leadership test scores for gifted and typical high school students. *Psychological Report*, 5, 713-717.

Cassity, J.H. (1925). Psychopathological glimpses of Lord Byron. *The Psychoan. Rev.*, 12, 397-413.

Cattell, J.M. and Brimhall, D.R. (1921). Families of American men of science. In American Men of Science, (3rd ed.), New York: Science Press.

Cattell, R.B. and Butcher, H.S. (1970). Creativity and personality. In P.E. Vernon (Ed.), *Creativity*, Baltimore: Penguin Books.

Christal, R.E. (1958). Factor analytic study of visual memory. *Psychol. Monogr.*, 72, No. 13.

Clark, B. (1979). Growing up gifted. Ohio, Columbus, Charles E. Meril, pp. 23-33.

Clark, B. (1988). Growing up gifted (3rd ed.). Columbus, OH: Charles E. Merrill.

Clark, B. (2002). *Growing up Gifted*, (6th ed.). New Jersey, Merrill Prentice Hall.

Cohler, M.J. (1941). Scholastic status of achievers and nonachievers of superior intelligence. *Journal of Educational Psychology*, 32, 603-610.

Colangelo, N. and Davis, G.A. (2003). *Introduction and Overview. In Handbook of Gifted Education*. 3rd ed., U.S.A. Pearson Education inc.

Colangelo, N. (1991). Counselling gifted students. In N. Colangelo and G.A. Davis (Eds.), *Handbook of Gifted Education* (pp. 273-284). Boston: Allyn and Bacon.

Colangelo, N. and Dettmann, D.F. (1983). A review of research on parents and families of gifted children. *Exceptional children*, 50(1), 20-27.

Coleman, J. (1962). *The Adolescent Society*. New York: Free Press.

Coleman, J.M. and Fultz, B.A. (1985). Special class placement, level of intelligence, and the self-concepts of gifted children: A social comparison perspective. *Remedial and Special Education*, 6(1), 7-12.

Coleman, L. (1985). Schooling the gifted. Reading, M.A.: Addison Wesley.

Cornell, D. and Grossberg, I. (1987). Family environment and personality adjustment in gifted programme children. *Gifted Child Quarterly*, 31(2), 59-64.

Cornish, R.C. (1968). Parents', Teachers', and pupils' perception of the gifted child's ability. *Gifted Child Quarterly*, 12, 14-17.

Covington, M., Crutchfield, R., Davies, L. and Olton, R. (1966). Productive thinking programme. Columbus, Ohio: Charles E. Merril.

Cox, Catharine C. (1926). The early mental traits of three hundred geniuses. Vol. II of Genetic Studies of Genius, Terman, L.M. (ed.). Stanford University Press.

Cross, T.L. (1997). Psychological and social aspects of educating gifted students. *Peabody Journal of Education*, 72(3 and 4), 180-200.

Crow, G.A. (1978). *Children at risk: A handbook of the signs and symptoms of early childhood difficulties*. New York: Shocken.

Davis, D. and Rimm, S. (1985). *Education of the Gifted*. Englewood Cliffs, NJ: Prentice-Hall.

Davis, G.A. (1973). *Psychology of Problem Solving: Theory and Practice*. New York: Basic Books.

Davis, G.A. and Rimm, S.B. (1994). *Education of Gifted and Talented* (3rd ed.). Needham Heights, MA: Allyn and Bacon.

Davis, G.A. and Rimm, S.B. (1989). *Education of the Gifted and Talented* (2nd ed.) Englewood Cliffs, NJ: Prentice-Hall.

Davis, W. (1953). Communicating science. *J. Atomic Scientists*, pp.337-340.

De Haan, R.T. (1964). Identifying gifted children. In J.L. French (ed.), *Educating the Gifted*. New York: Holt, Rinehart and Winston.

Dearborn, G.V. (1998). A study in imagination. *Amer. J. Psychol.*, 9, 183-190.

Delisle, J. (1981). The non-productive gifted child: A contradiction of terms? *Roeper Review*, 3, 20-22.

Delisle, J. (1982). The gifted underachievers: Learning to underachieve. *Roeper Review*, 4, 16-18.

Delisle, J. (1994). Dealing with the stereotype of underachievement. *Gifted Child Today*, 17(6), 20-21.

Delisle, J.R. and Renzulli J.S. (1982). The revolving door identification and programming model: Correlates of creative production. *Gifted Children Quarterly*, 26(2), 89-95.

Department of Education (1993). Resource document: The education of gifted students. Brisbane, Old: Department of Education.

Dewey, J. (1910). How we think. Boston: Heath.

Dictionary of Occupational Titles, Part I (1949) (2nd ed.). Washington, D.C. United Stats Government Printing Office.

Dougherty, M.L. (1956). School acceleration. The Educational Clinics of the Department of Education. The John Hopkins University, pp. 42-51.

Dreary, I.J. (2000). *Looking down on intelligence: From Psychometrics to the brain.* Oxford University Press.

Eby, J.W. and Smutny, J.F. (1990). A thoughtful overview of gifted education. New York: Longman.

Ellis, H.A. (1926). *A study of British genius* (Rev. ed.) Boston: Houghton Mifflin.

ERIC Clearinghouse on Disabilities and Gifted Education,http:// www.kidsource.com/kidsource/ content/giftedness_and_gifted.html accessed on 11/4/04.

Erikson, E.H. (1950). *Childhood and Society*. New York: Norton.

Falbo, T. and Cooper, C. (1980). Young Children's time and intellectual ability. *Journal of Genetic Psychology*, 137(2), 299-300.

Feldhusen, J.F. (1995). Talent development during the high school years. *Gifted Education International*, 10, 60-64.

Feldhusen, J.F. and Kolloff, M.B. (1978). A three stage model for gifted education. *Gifted/Creative/Talented*, 4, 3-5, 53-57.

Feldhusen, J.F. and Kroll, M.D. (1985). Parent perceptions of gifted children's educational needs. *Roeper Review*, 7(4), 249-252.

Feldhusen, J.F., Proctor, T.B. and Black, K.N. (1986). Guidelines for grade advancement of precocious children. *Roeper Review*, 9, 25-27.

Feldman, D.H. (1984). A follow-up of subjects scoring about 180 IQ in Terman's "Genetic Studies of Genius." *Exceptional children*, 50(6) 518-523.

Fliegler, L.A. (1961). *Curriculum Planning for the Gifted*. Englewood Cliffs, N.J.: Prentice-Hall.

Fliegler, L.A. and Bish, C.E. (1959). The gifted and talented. *Rev. ed. Res.*, 29, 408-450.

Fox, L.H. (1979). Programmes for the gifted and talented: An overview. In A.H. Passow (Ed), The 78th Yearbook of the National Society for the Study of Education, Part 1, The gifted and talented: Their education and development. Chicago: University of Chicago Press.

Franks, B. and Dolan, L. (1982). Affecting characteristics of gifted children: Educational implications. *Gifted Child Quarterly*, 26, 172-178.

Freeman, F.N. (1924). The treatment of the gifted child in the light of scientific evidence. *Elementary School Journal*, Vol. XXIV, May, pp. 652-661.

Freeman, J. (1994). Some emotional aspects of being gifted. *Journal for the Education of the Gifted*, 17(2), 180-197.

Frierson, E.C. (1965). Upper and lower status gifted children: A study of difference. *Exceptional Children*. 32, 83-90.

Fulgosi, A. and Guilford, J.P. (1970). Short-term incubation in divergent production. *Journal of Creative Behaviour*, 4, 131-132.

Fund for the Advancement of Education (1957). They went to college early. *Education Report No.* 2. New York: Author.

Gagne, F. (1985). Giftedness and talent: Re-examining a re-examination of the definitions. *Gifted Child Quarterly*, 29, 103-112.

Gagne, F. (1995). From giftedness to talent: A developmental model and its impact on the field. *Roeper Review*, 18(2), 103-111.

Galbraith, J. (1985). The eight great gripes of gifted kids: Responding to special needs. *Roeper Review*, 7, 16.

Gallagher, J. (1966). Research Summary on gifted child education. Springfield, IL: Office of the Superintendent of Public Instruction.

Gallagher, J.J. and Crowder, T.H. (1957). Adjustment of gifted children in the regular classroom. *Exceptional children*, 23, 306-312, 317-319.

Gallagher, J.J. (1958). Social status of children related to intelligence, propinquity, and social perception. *Elementary School Journal*, 58, 225-231.

Gallagher, J.J. (1975). *Teaching the Gifted Child* (1st and 2nd ed.). Boston: Allyn & Bacon.

Gallagher, J.J. (1979). Issues in education for the gifted. In A.H. Passow (Ed.). The 78th Yearbook of the National Society for the study of Education, Part I, The gifted and talented: Their education and development. Chicago: University of Chicago Press.

Gallagher, J.J. (1985). *Teaching the Gifted Child* (3rd ed.). Boston: Allyn & Bacon.

Gallagher, J.J. (1988). National agenda for educating gifted students: Statement of priorities. *Exceptional Children* 55, 107-114.

Galton, F. (1869). *Hereditary Genius*. London: Macmillan.

Gardner, H. (1983). *Frames of Mind: The Theory of Multiple Intelligences*. New York: Basic Books.

Gardner, H. (1993). Multiple intelligences: The theory in practice. New York: Basic Books.

Gardner, H. and Hatch, T. (1989). Multiple intelligences go to school: Educational implications of the theory of multiple intelligences. *Educational Researcher*, 18(8), 4-9.

Gear, G. (1975). Effects of the training programme, Identification of the Potentially Gifted, on teachers' accuracy in the identification of intellectually gifted children. (Doctoral dissertation, University of Connecticut, 1975). *Dissertation Abstracts International*, 1976, 36, 6548 (University Microfilms No. DAH76-07183).

Gear, G. (1976). A survey of teacher judgement in identifying intellectually gifted children: A review of the literature. *Gifted Child Quarterly*, 20, 478-489.

Gear, G. (1978). Effects of training on teachers' accuracy in the identification of gifted children. *Gifted Child Quarterly*, 22, 90-97.

Geortzel, V. and Geortzel, M.G. (1962). *Cradles of Eminence.* Boston: Little, Brown.

Getzels, J.W. and Dillon, J.T. (1973). The nature of giftedness and the education of the gifted child. In R. Travers (Ed.), Second handbook of research on teaching. Chicago: Rand Mc Nally.

Gist, A.S. (1917). Acceleration of pupils. *School and Society*, Vol. V, January 17, pp. 116-118.

Gold, M. (1979). Acceleration: Simplistic gimmickry. In W. George (Eds.), *Educating the Gifted: Acceleration and Enrichment.* Baltimore: Johns Hopkins University Press.

Goleman, D. (1980). 1,528 little geniuses and how they grew. *Psychology Today*, 13(9), 28-43.

Good, H.G. (1960). *A History of Western Education* (2nd ed.). New York: Macmillan.

Goodhart, B.F. and Schmidt, S.D. (1940). Educational Characteristics of superior Children. *Baltimore Bulletin of Education*, Vol. 18, September, pp. 14-17.

Gottfried, A.E. and Gottfried, A.W. (1996). A longitudinal study of academic intrinsic motivation in intellectually gifted children: Childhood through early adolescence. *Gifted Child Quarterly*, 40(4), 179-183.

Gowan, J.C. (1955). The underachieving gifted child – A problem for everyone. *Exceptional Children*, 21 April, 247-249, 270-271.

Gowan, J.C. (1960). Factors of achievement in high school and college. J. *Counsel. Psychol.*, 7, 91-95.

Greenspon, T.S. (2000). The self-experience of the gifted person: Theory and definitions. *Roeper Review*, 22(3) 176-181.

Gross, M.V.M. (2000). Issues in the cognitive development of exceptionally and profoundly gifted individuals (pp.179-192). In K.A. Heller, Monks, F.J. and Passow, A.H. (Eds.), *International Handbook of Research and Development of Giftedness and Talent* (2nd ed.). (pp. 179-192). Amsterdam: Elsevier.

Grost, A. (1970). Genius in residence. Englewood Cliffs, NJ: Prentice Hall.

Grotberg, E.H. (1965). Adjustment problems of the gifted. In W.B. Barbe, *Psychology and Education of the Gifted: Selected Readings.* New York, Appleton-Century-Crofts.

Guilford, J.P. (1950). Creativity. *American Psychologist*, 5, 444-454.

Guilford, J.P. (1956a). Les dimensions de intellect. In H. Laugier (Ed.), L'analyse factorielle et ses applications. Paris: Centre National de la Recherche Scientifique, pp. 53-74.

Guilford, J.P. (1956b). The structure of intellect. *Psyho. Bull.*, 53, 267-293.

Guilford, J.P. (1958). New Frontiers of testing in the discovery and development of human talent. In seventh Annual Western Regional Conference on Testing problems. Los Angeles: Educational Testing Service, pp. 20-32.

Guilford, J.P. (1967). The nature of human intelligence. London, Mc Graw-Hill Book Company.

Guilford, J.P. (1988). Some changes in the structure of intellect model. *Educational and Psychological Measurement*, 48, 1-4.

Hackney, H. (1981). The gifted child, the family, and the school. *Gifted Child Quarterly*, 25, 51-54.

Hagen, E. (1980). Identification of the gifted. New York: Teacher College Press.

Haggard, E.A. (1957). Socialization, personality and academic achievement in gifted children. *School Review*, 65, December, pp. 388-414.

Hallahan, D.P. and Kauffman, J.M. (1991). *Exceptional Children: Introduction to Special Education*. Boston, Allyn and Bacon.

Havighurst, R.J. (1962). Growing up in river city. New York: John Wiley.

Hein, S. (2004). History and definition of emotional intelligence, eqi.org/history.htm

Higham S.J. and Buescher, T.M. (1987). What young gifted adolescents understand about feeling different. In T.M. Buescher (Ed.) Understanding gifted and talented adolescents: A resource guide for counsellors, educators, and parents (pp.26-30). Evanston, IL: Centre for Talent Development, North-western University.

Highsmith, J.A. (1925). Relation of the rate of response to intelligence. *Psychol. Rev. Monogr.*, 34, 1-33.

Hitchfield, E.M. (1973). *In Search of Promise*. London: Longman.

Hocevar, D. (1980). Intelligence, divergent thinking, and creativity. *Intelligence*, 4, 25-40.

Hoge, R.D. and Renzulli, J.S. (1993). Exploring the link between giftedness and self-concept. *Review of Educational Research*, 63, 449-465.

Hollingworth, L.S. (1923). *Special Talents and Defects: Their Significance for Education*. New York: Macmillan.

Hollingworth, L.S. (1926). Gifted children: Their nature and nurture. New York: Macmillan.

Hollingworth, L.S. (1931). How should gifted children be educated? *Baltimore Bulletin of Education*, 50, 196.

Hollingworth, L.S. (1942). *Children above 180 IQ, Stanford-Binet: Origin and Development*. New York: World Book Company.

Holt, J. (1969). *The Underachieving School*. New York: Dell.

Horrall, B.M. (1957). Academic performance and personality adjustments of highly intelligent college students. *Genetic Psychology Monographs*, 55, February, pp. 3-83.

Howley, A., Howley, C. and Pendarvis, E. (1986). Teaching gifted children: Principles and strategies. Boston: Little, Brown.

http://sp.uconn.edu/~nrcgt/sem/semexcl.html accessed on 2/20/04.

http://www.ed.gov/pubs/Tools for Schools/sem.html accessed on 12/24/04.

http://www.growing-up.com/parenting-gifted.html accessed on 12/24/04.

http://www.ri.net/gifted/talented/character.htmlaccessed on 12/24/04.

Irvine, Paul (2000). Terman, Lewis M. (1877-1956), in *Encyclopaedia of Special Education* (2nd ed.), Vol. 3. Edited by Reynolds, C.R. and Janzen, E.F., John Wiley & Sons, New York, p. 1781.

Jacobs, J.C. (1971). Effectiveness of teacher and parent identification of gifted children as a function of school level. *Psychology in the schools*, 8, 140-142.

Janos, P.M. and Robinson, N.M. (1985). *Psychological Development in Intellectually Gifted Children.* In F.D. Horowitz and M. O' Brien (Eds.), The gifted and talented: Developmental perspectives (pp.149-195). Washington, DC: American Psychological Association.

Johnson, D. and Johnson, R. (1987). The achieving student in heterogeneous cooperative learning groups. *Paper developed for a workshop at the University of Minnesota.*

Johnson, D.M. (1955). The psychology of thought and judgement. New York: Harper & Row.

Johnson, H.G. (1942). Does the gifted child have a low IQ? *Journal of Educational Research*, 36, 91-99.

Johnson, O.J. (1923). Teachers' judgements of qualities of gifted pupils as related to classroom activities. *School and Society*, 17, 466-469.

Jones, A.M. (1925). An analytical study of one hundred and twenty superior children. *Psychological Clinic*, 16, 19-76.

Jones, E.E. (1912). Suggestions from cases of unusually rapid or irregular progress in public schools. *Proceedings of the National Education Association for 1912*, pp. 640-645.

Jones, K. and Day, J.D., (1996). Cognitive similarities between academically and socially gifted students. *Gifted Child Quarterly*, 18(4), 270-273.

Jordan, J.B. (1974). Foundation for exceptional children address the needs of the culturally gifted child. *Exceptional Children*, 40, 279-283.

Karnes, M., Shwedel, A. and Steinberg, D. (1984). Styles of parenting among parents of young gifted children. *Roeper Review*, 6(4), 232-235.

Keating, D.P. (1974). The study of mathematically precocious youth. In J.C. Stanley, D.P. Keating, and L.H. Fox (Eds.), *Mathematical Talent: Discovery, Description and Development*. Baltimore: Johns Hopkins University Press.

Ketcham, B. and Snyder, R.T. (1977). Self attitude of the intellectually and socially advantaged students. *Psychological Reports*, 40, 111-116.

Keys, N. (1938). The underage student in high school and college. Publ. Educ., Univ. California.

Khatena, J. (1982). Educational Psychology for the gifted. New York: John Wiley.

Kirk, W.D. (1966). A tentative screening procedure for bright and slow children in kindergarten. *Exceptional Children*, 33, 235-240.

Kirschenbaum, R.J. (1983). Let's cut out the cut-off score in the identification of the gifted. Roeper Review: *A Journal on Gifted Education*, 5, 6-10.

Kirschenbaum, R.J. and Siegle, D. (1993). Predicting creative performance in an enrichment programme. Paper presented at the Association for the Education of Gifted Underachieving Students, 6th Annual Conference, April, Portland, OR.

Kitano, M., and Kirby, D. (1986). *Gifted Education: A Comparative View*. Boston: Little Brown.

Kohlberg, L. (1984). *The Psychology of Moral Development*. New York: Harper & Row.

Kos, R. (1993). "Nobody knows my life but me!" The story of Ben, a reading disabled adolescent. In R. Donmeyer and R. Kos (ed.) *At-risk Students: Portraits, Policies, Programmes, and Practices*. Albany, NY: State University of New York Press, pp. 49-78.

Krugman, M. (1960). Identifying and preservation of talent. *Teachers Coll. Rec.*, 61, 459-463.

Krutch, J.W. (1926). Edgar Allan Poe, *A Study in Genius*. New York: Alfred A. Knopf, p. 245.

Kulik, J.A. and Kulik, C.C. (1991). Research on acceleration. In N. Colangelo & G.A. Davis (Eds.), *Handbook of Gifted Education*. Boston: Allyn & Bacon.

Kulik, J.A. and Kulik, C.-L.C. (1984). Effects of accelerated instruction on students. *Review of Educational Research*, 54, 409-425.

Lange-Eichbaum, W. (1932). *The Problem of Genius*. New York. Macmillan.

Lashaway-Bokina, N. (2000). Recognizing and nurturing intrinsic motivation: A cautionary tale. *Roeper Review*, 22(4), 225-227.

Laycock, F. (1979). Gifted children. Glenview, IL: Scott, Foresman.

Laycock, F. and Caylor, J.S. (1964). Physiques of gifted children and their siblings. *Child Development*, 35, 63-74.

Learned, W.S. and Wood, B.D. (1938). The student and his knowledge. Carnegie Found. *Adv. Teaching Bull.*, No. 29.

Leaverton, L. and Herzog, S. (1979). Adjustment of the gifted child. *Journal for the Education of the Gifted*, 2(3), 149-152.

Lehman, H.C. (1953). *Age and Achievement*. Princeton: Princeton Univ. Press.

Levinson, B.M. (1956). Rethinking the selection of intellectually gifted children. *Psychol. Rep.*, 2, 127-130.

Lightfoot, G. (1951). Personality characteristics of bright and dull children: contributions to education (No 969). New York: Teachers College, Columbia University.

Lock, R. and Jay, G. (1987). Self-concept in gifted children: Differential impact in boys and girls. *Gifted Child Quarterly*, 31, 9-14.

Lombroso, C. (1905). *The Man of Genius* (2nd ed.). New York: Walter-Scott.

Luftig, R.L. and Nichols, M.N. (1991). An assessment of the social status and perceived personality and school traits of gifted students by non-gifted peers. *Roeper Review*, 13(3), 148-153.

Mac Kinnon, D.W. (1962). The nature and nurture of creative talent. *American Psychologist*, 17, 484-495.

Maker, C.J. and Schiever, S.W. (1989). Defining the hispanic population. In C.J. Maker and S.W. Schiever (Eds.), Critical issues in gifted education: Defensible programmes for cultural and ethnic minorities (Vol. 2), (pp. 1-4). Austin, TX: Pro-Ed.

Maker, C.J. (1986). Education of the gifted: Significant trends. In R.J. Morris and B. Blatt (Eds.), *Special Education: Research and Trends* (pp. 190-221). New York: Pergamon.

Makers, J. (1925). Genius and disaster: Studies in drugs and genius. New York: Adelphi Company.

Marland, S.P. (1972). Education of the gifted and talented. (2 vols.). Report to congress of the United States Commissioner of Education. Washington, DC: US Government Printing Office.

Martens, E.H. (1951). Gifted children: What do we know about them? What shall we do about them? *The Nation's Schools*, June, p. 33.

Martinson, R.A. (1972). Research on the gifted and talented: Its implications for education. In S. Marland, Jr. (Ed.), Education of the gifted and talented. Report to the congress of the United States by the U.S. Commissioner of Education, Washington, DC: U.S. Government Printing Office.

Martinson, R.A. (1973). The identification of the gifted and talented. Washington, DC: National Clearinghouse on the Gifted and Talented, (mimeo).

Martinson, R.A. (1976). A guide toward better teaching for the gifted. Ventura, Calif.: Office of the Ventura County Superintendent of Schools.

Martinson, R.A. and Lessinger, L.M. (1960). Problems in the identification of intellectually gifted pupils. *Exceptional Children*, 26, 227-242.

Maslow, A. (1968). *Toward a Psychology of Being* (2nd ed.). New York: Van Nostrand Reinhold.

Maslow, A. (1971). *The Father Reaches of Human Nature*. New York: Viking.

Mayer, Salovey, P. and Caruso. eqi.org/history. htm accessed on 12-10-04.

Mc Elwee, E.W. (1932). A comparison of the personality traits of 300 accelerated, normal and retarded children. *Journal of Educational Research*, Vol. XXVI, September, pp. 31-34.

Mc Ginn, P.V. (1976). Verbally gifted youth: Selection and description. In D.P. Keating (Ed.), *Intellectual Talent: Research and Development*. Baltimore: John Hopkins University.

Mensch, I. (1950). Rorschach study of the gifted child. *Exceptional Children*, 17, 8-14.

Merrifield, P.R. *et al.* (1962). The role of intellectual factors in problem solving. *Psychol. Monogr.*, 76, No. 10.

Miles, C.C. (1954). Gifted children, in L. Carmichael, ed., *Manual of Child Psychology*, New York: John Wiley.

Milgram, R.M. and Milgram, N.A. (1976). Personality characteristics of gifted Israeli Children. *Journal of Genetic Psychology*, 129, 185-194.

Miller, L.M. (Ed.) (1961). Guidance for the underachiever with superior ability. Washington, DC: U.S. Government Printing Office.

Miller, V. (1957). Academic achievement and social adjustment of children young for their grade placement. *Elementary School Journal*, 57, 257-263.

Monahan, J.E. and Hollingworth, L.S. (1927). Neuromuscular capacity of children who test above 135 IQ (Stanford-Binet). *Journal of Educational Psychology*, 18, 88-96.

Moon, S.M., Kelly, K.R. and Feldhusen, J.F. (1997). Specialized counselling services for gifted youth and their families: A needs assessment. *Gifted Child Quarterly*, 41, 16-25.

navodaya.nic.in/jnvs.htm accessed on 28/6/05.

navodaya.nic.in/Lateral Entry. htm accessed on 28/6/05.

Neisser, U. (1979). The concept of intelligence. In R.J. Sternberg and D.K. Dotterman (Eds.), Human—Intelligence (pp. 179-189). Norwood, NJ: Ablex.

Newland, T.E. (1976). The gifted in socio educational perspective. Englewood Cliffs, NJ: Prentice Hall.

Northwest Regional Educational Laboratory (2000, September 11). Differentiating Processes [On-Line]. Available: http://www.nwrel.org/msec/just _good/9/chg. Html [2001, June].

O'Leary, M.J. (1955). The measurement and evaluation of the work habits of overachievers and underachievers to determine the relationship of these habits to achievement. Doctoral dissertation (Boston: Boston University) *Abstract in Dissertation Abstracts*, 15, 2104-2105.

Oden, M.H. (1968). The fulfilment of promise: 40 year follow-up of the Terman gifted group. *Genetic Psychology Monographs*, 77, 3-93.

Olszewski, P. Kulieke, M. and Buescher, T. (1987). The influence of the family environment on the development of talent: A literature review. *Journal for the Education of the Gifted*, 8, 9-23.

Olszewski-Kubilius, P., Kulieke, M. and Krasney, N. (1988). Personality dimensions of gifted adolescents: A review of the empirical literature. *Gifted Child Quarterly*, 32(4), 347-352.

Olton, R.M. (1979). Experimental studies of incubation: searching the elusive. *Journal of Creative Behaviour*, 13, 9-22.

Oram, G.D., Dewey, D.G. and Rutemiller, L.A. (1995). Relations between academic aptitude and psychosocial adjustment in gifted programme students. *Gifted Child Quarterly*, 39(4), 236-244.

Orlosky, D.E. and Smith, B.O. (1978). Curriculum development: Issues and insights. Chicago: Rand Mc Nally College Publishing.

Parker, W.D. and Adkins, K.K. (1995). Perfectionism and the gifted. *Roeper Review*, 17(3), 173-176.

Parkyn, G.W. (1948). Children of high intelligence: A New Zealand study. Wellington, N.Z.: Council for Educational Research.

Patrick, C. (1935). Creative thought in poets. *Arch. Psychol.*, New York, 26, 1-74.

Patrick, C. (1938). Scientific thought. *Journal of Psychology*, 5, 55-83.

Peabody, J. (1991). Origins of despair. *Unpublished paper.*

Pegnato, C.W. and Birch, J.W. (1959). Locating gifted children in junior high schools; a comparison of methods, Exceptional Children 25, 300-304.

Perkins, D. (1995). Outsmarting IQ: The emerging science of learnable intelligence. New York: The Free Press.

Petrosko, J.M. (1978). Measuring creativity in elementary school: The current state of the art. *Journal of Creative Behaviour*, 12(2), 109-119.

Piechowski, M.M. (1991). Emotional development and emotional giftedness. In N. Colangelo and G.A. Davis (Eds.), Handbook of gifted education (pp. 285-306). Needham Heights, MA: Allyn & Bacon.

Pippart, R., and Archer, N.A. (1963). A comparison of two methods for classifying underachievers with respect to selected criteria. *Personnel and Guidance Journal*, 41, 788-791.

Plowman, P., and Rice, J. (1967). Final report: California Project Talent. Sacramento: California Department of Public Instruction.

Plucker, J., and Mc Intir, J. (1995). Academic survivability in high ability, middle school students. *Gifted Child Quarterly*.

Pohl, R. (1970). Teacher nomination of intellectually gifted children in the primary grades. (Doctoral dissertation, University of Illinois at Urbana). *Dissertation Abstracts International,* 31, 2237. (University Microfilms No. 70-21037).

Poincare, H. (1913). The foundations of science. New York: Science Press.

Pressey, S. (1955). Concerning the nature and nurture of genius. *Science*, 31, 123-129.

Pressey, S.L. (1949). Educational acceleration: Appraisals and basic problems. Columbus: Ohio State University Press.

Pressey, S.L. (1955). Concerning the nature and nurture of genius. *Scientific Monthly*, 81, 124.

Pressey, S.L. (1963). Acceleration and the gifted. Columbus, Ohio: Ohio State *Department of Education*, p.1-4.

Purkey, W. (1966). Measured and professed personality characteristics of gifted high school students and analysis of their congruence. *Journal of Educational Research*, 3, 99-103.

Ralph, J.B. Goldberg, M.L. and Passow, A.H. (1966). Bright underachievers. New York: Teachers College Press.

Ramaseshan, P. (1957). The social and emotional adjustment of the gifted (Doctoral Dissertation, University of Nebraska). *Dissertation Abstract International*, 17, 1267 (University Microfilms No.100-20993).

Ramos-Ford, V., and Gardner, H. (1997). Giftedness from a multiple intelligences perspective. In N. Colangelo and G.A. Davis (Eds.), Handbook of gifted education (2nd ed., pp.54-66). Boston: Allyn & Bacon.

Renzulli, J. (1973). New directions in creativity, New York: Harper & Row.

Renzulli, J.S. (1971). Talent potentials in minority group students. *Exceptional Children*, 38, 437-444.

Renzulli, J.S. (1978). What makes giftedness? A reexamination of the definition of the gifted and talented. Storrs, Conn.: University of Connecticut, (mimeo) (*a*).

Renzulli, J.S. (1986). The three ring conception of giftedness: A developmental model for creative productivity. In R.J. Sternberg and J.E. Davidson (Eds.), Conceptions of giftedness (pp. 53-92). New York, Cambridge University Press.

Renzulli, J.S. (1994). Schools for talent development: A practical plan for total school improvement. Melbourne, Vic: Hawker Brownlow Education.

Renzulli, J.S. and Reis, S.M. (1997). The schooliwde enrichment model: A how-to guide for educational excellence. Mansfield Centre. CT: Creative Learning Press.

Renzulli, J.S. and Delcourt, M.A.B. (1986). The legacy and logic of research on identification of gifted persons. *Gifted Child Quarterly*, 30, 20-23.

Renzulli, J.S. and Reis, S.M. (1985). The schoolwide enrichment model: A comprehensive plan for educational excellence. Mansfield Centre CT: Creative Learning Press.

Renzulli, J.S. and Reis, S.M. The schoolwide enrichment model executive Summary. http://sp. uconn.edu/~nrcgt/sem/semexec.html accessed on 12-12-04.

Renzulli, J.S. and Smith, L.H. (1977). Two approaches to identification of gifted students. *Exceptional Children*, 43, 512-518.

Renzulli, J.S., Reis, S.M. and Smith, L.H. (1981). The revolving door identification model. Mansfield Centre CT: Creative Learning Press.

Renzulli, J.S., Smith, L.H., White, A.J., Callaham, C.M. and Hartman, R.K. (1976). Scales for rating the behavioural characteristics of superior students. Wethersfield, conn.: Creative Learning Press.

Reynolds, M. (Ed.) (1962). Early school admission for mentally advanced children. Reston, VA: Council for Exceptional Children.

Rimland, B. (1964). Infantile autism. New York: Appleton-Century-Crofts.

Rimm, S. and Lowe, B. (1988). Family environments of underachieving gifted students. *Gifted Child Quarterly*, 32, 353-359.

Rimm, S.B. (1986). Underachievement syndrome: Causes and cures. Watertown Wl: Apple.

Robinson, H.B., Roedell, W.C. and Jackson, N.E. (1979). Early identification and intervention. In A.H. Passow (Ed.), The 78th Yearbook of the National Society for the Study of Education, Part 1, The gifted and talented: Their education and development. Chicago: University of Chicago Press.

Roe, A. (1953). The making of a scientist. New York: Dodd Mead.

Roedell, W. (1984). Vulnerabilities of highly gifted children. *Roeper Review*, 6(3), 127-130.

Roeper, A. (1992). Characteristics of gifted children and how parents and teacher can cope with them. *Roeper Review*, 11, 31-32.

Roeper, A.M. http://www.growing-up.com/parenting_ gifted.html accessed on 03-20-05.

Roesslein, C.G. (1953). Differential patterns of intelligence traits between high achieving and low achieving high school boys. Washington, DC: Catholic University of America Press.

Sackett, C.H. (1929). The later success of accelerated pupils. Junior-Senior High School Clearing House, Vol. IV, September, pp. 22-27.

Sandor, B. (1932). The functioning of memory and the methods of mathematical prodigies. *Charact. & Pers.*, 1, 70-74.

Sankaranarayanam, Arun (2003). What is intelligence? Assessment standards and criteria. *The Hindu.*

Sarason, S.B. and Gladwin, T. (1958). Psychological culture problems in mental subnormality: a review of research. *Genet. Psychol. Monogr.,* 57, 3-289.

Satir, V. (1972). Peoplemaking. Palo Alto, CA: Science & Behaviour Books.

Scheerer, M., Rothmann, E. and Goldstein, K. (1945). A case of "idiot savant": an experimental study of personality organization. *Psychol. Monogr.*, 58, 4.

Scheme to bring talented dropouts back to school (2005), *The Hindu*, 11 May.

Schlowinski, E. and Reynolds, C.R. (1985). Dimensions of anxiety among high IQ Children. *Gifted Child Quarterly*, 29(3), 125-130.

Sears, P.S. (1979). The Terman genetic studies of genius, 1922-1972. In A.H. Passow (Ed.), The gifted and the talented (pp. 75-96). Chicago: National Society for the Study of Education.

Sears, P.S. and Barbee, A.M. (1977). Career and life satisfaction among Terman's gifted women. In J.C. Stanley, W.C. George, and C.H. Solano (Eds.), The gifted and the creative: A fifty-year perspective (pp.28-65). Baltimore: Johns Hopkins University Press.

Sears, R.R. (1977). Sources of life satisfaction of the Terman gifted men. *American Psychologist*, 32, 119-128.

Seeley, K. (1993). Gifted students at risk. In L. Silverman (ed.), Counselling the gifted and talented. Denver: Love Publishing.

Sellin, D. and Birch, J. (1980). Educating gifted and talented learners. Rockville, M.D.: Aspen.

Sewis, W.D. (1940). A study of superior children in the elementary school. Nashville: Cullom and Ghertner.

Shanie, Josh (2004) www.geocities.com/Athens/crete/1019/Interests/Potenial.html.

Shannon, D.C. (1957). What research says about acceleration. Phi Delta Kappan, 39, 70-73.

Sharma, J.C. (1988). National Talent Search: The scheme and a critical appraisal of its tools. New Delhi, National Council of Educational Research and Training, pp. 243-260.

Shaw, M.C., II and Brown, D.J. (1957). Scholastic underachievement of bright college students. *Personnel and Guidance Journal*, 36, 195-199.

Silverman, L.K. (1991). Helping gifted girls reach their potential. Roeper Review, 13(3), 122-123.

Silverman, L.K. (1994). The moral sensitivity of gifted children and the evolution of society. *Roeper Review*, 17(2), 110-116.

Silverman, L.K. in Vizas, Kyra, Parenting your gifted child, http://www.growing_up.com/parenting_gifted. html accessed on 3/20/05.

Silverman, Y. and Jones, V. (1932). A study of early entrance to college. The Journal of Educational Psychology, Vol. XXIII, January, pp. 58-72.

Sisk, D.A. (1988). Children at risk: The identification of the gifted among the minority. *Gifted Education International*, 5, 138-141.

Sizer, T. (1992). Horace's School. Boston: Houghton Mifflin.

Solano, D.H. and George, W.C. (1976). College courses for the gifted. Gifted Child Quarterly, 20(3), 274-285.

Southern, W.T., Jones, E.D. and Fiscus, E.D. (1989). Practitioner objections to the academic acceleration of gifted children. *Gifted Child Quarterly*, 33(1), 29-35.

Spearman, C. (1927). The abilities of man. New York: Macmillan.

Specht, L.F. (1919). A Terman class in public school no.64. Manhattan, *School and Society*, 9, 393-398.

Spencer, H. (1895). The principles of psychology. (3rd ed.), New York: Appleton.

Stallings, C. (1972). Gifted disadvantaged children. Technical paper, National Leadership Institute Teacher Education-Early Childhood. Storrs, Conn.: University of Connecticut.

Stanley, J.C. (1976). Concern for intellectually talented youths: How it originated and fluctuated. *Journal of Clinical Child Psychology*, 5, 38-42.

Starko, A.J. (1986). It's about time: Inservice strategies for curriculum compacting. Mansfield Centre, CT: Creative Learning Press.

Stephens, K. (1996). Product development for gifted students. *Gifted Child Today Magazine*, 19, November-December, pp. 18-20.

Stern, W. (1911). The supernormal child. *Journal of Educational Psychology*, 2, 71-75.

Sternberg, R. (1985). Beyond IQ: A triarchic theory of human intelligence. Cambridge, England: Cambridge University Press.

Sternberg, R. (2000). Patterns of giftedness: A triarchic analysis. *Roeper Review*, 22, 231-240.

Sternberg, R. and Wagner, R. (1982). A revolutionary look at intelligence. *Gifted Children Newsletter*, 3, 11.

Sternberg, R.J. (1984). Toward a triarchic theory of human intelligence. *Behavioural and Brain Sciences*, 7, 269-287.

Sternberg, R.S. (1986). A triarchic theory in intellectual giftedness. In R.S. Sternberg and R.E. Davidson (Eds.), Conceptions of giftedness. Cambridge: Cambridge University Press.

Stouffer, S.A. and Shea, P.D. (1959). Your educational plans. Chicago: Science Research Associates.

Strang, R. (1960). Mental hygiene of gifted children. *The Gifted Child*, pp. 131-162.

Study of the progress of under-age pupils at Milton, Massachusetts (1931). *American School Board Journal*, Vol. LXXXIII, November, p. 34.

Supplee, P.L. (1990). Reaching the underachiever: Programme strategy and design. New York: Teachers College Press.

Sutherland, A. and Goldsmith, M.L. (1974). Negative Teacher expectation and change in children with superior intellectual potential. *Child Development*, 45, 852-856.

Tannenbaum, A.H. (1962). Adolescent attitudes towards academic brilliance. New York: Bureau of Publications, Teachers College, Columbia University.

Tannenbaum, A.J. (1979). Pre-Sputnik to post Watergate concern about the gifted. In A.H. Passow (Ed.), The gifted and the talented (pp. 5-27). Chicago: National Society for the Study of Education.

Tannenbaum, A.J. (1983). Gifted Children: Psychological and Educational Perspectives. New York: Macmillan.

Tannenbaum, A.J. (2003). Nature and nurture of giftedness. In N. Colangelo and G.A. Davis (Eds.), Handbook of gifted education, (3rd ed.). Boston: Allyn & Bacon.

Taylor, C. (1968). The multiple talent approach. *Instructor*, 77, 142-146.

Taylor, R.L. and Sternberg, L. (1989). Exceptional Children: Integrating research and training. New York, Springer-Verlag.

Telford, C.W. and Sawrey, J.M. (1977). The exceptional individual, New Jersey, Prentice-Hall, Inc., Englewood Cliffs.

Tempest, N.R. (1974). Teaching clever children 7-11. Boston: Routledge & Kegan Paul.

Terman, L.M. (1904). A preliminary study in the psychology and pedagogy of leadership. Pedag. Sem., 11, 413-451.

Terman, L.M. (1906). Genius and stupidity: A study of some of the intellectual processes of seven "Bright" and seven "Dull" boys. Pedag. Sem. 13, 307-373.

Terman, L.M. (1917). The intelligence quotient of Francis Galton in Childhood. *Amer. J. Psychol.* 28, 209-215.

Terman, L.M. (1925). *Genetic Studies of Genius*. Palo Alto: Stanford University Press.

Terman, L.M. (1926). Genetic studies of genius, Vol. 1: Mental and physical traits of a thousand gifted children (2nd ed.). Palo Alto, CA: Stanford University Press.

Terman, L.M. (1954). Scientists and non-scientists in a group of 800 gifted men. *Psychol. Monogr.* 68.

Terman, L.M. (Ed.) *et al.* (1925). Mental and Physical traits of a thousand gifted children. Vol. 1 of Genetic studies of genius, Terman, L.M. (ed.). Stanford: Stanford University Press.

Terman, L.M. and Oden, M.H. (1947). Genetic studies of genius: Vol. 4. The gifted child grows up. Stanford: Stanford University Press.

Terman, L.M. and Oden, M.H. (1951). The Stanford studies of the gifted. In P.A. Witty (Ed.), The gifted child. Boston: D.C. Heath.

Terman, L.M. and Oden, M.H. (1959). Genetic studies of genius: Vol. 5. The gifted group at midlife: Thirty-five year's follow-up of a superior group. Stanford: Stanford University Press.

Terman, L.M., Burks, B.S. and Jensen, D.W. (1930). Genetic studies of genius.

Vol. 3. The promise of youth: Follow-up studies of a thousand gifted children. Stanford, CA: Stanford University Press.

The intelligence of Scottish children (1933). Scottish Council for Research in Education. London: University of London Press.

Thom, D.A. and Newell, N. (1945). Hazards of the high IQ. Mental Hygiene, January, pp. 61-77.

Thorndike, E.L. (1920). Intelligence and its uses. Harper's Mag., 140, 227-235.

Thorndike, E.L. (1921). Intelligence and its measurement. *Journal of Educational Psychology*, 12, 127.

Thurstone, L.L. (1938). Primary mental abilities. Chicago University Press.

Torrance, E.P. (1962). *Guiding Creative Talent*, Englewood Cliffs, NJ: Prentice-Hall.

Torrance, E.P. (1964). Identifying the creatively gifted among disadvantaged children. *Gifted Child Quarterly*, 8, 171-176.

Torrance, E.P. (1966). Torrance Tests of creative thinking. Lexington, Mass.: Personnel Press.

Torrance, E.P. (1969). Creative positives of disadvantaged youth. *Gifted Child Quarterly*, 13, 71-81.

Torrance, E.P. (1973). Assessment of disadvantaged minority group children. *School Psychology Digest*, 2, 3-10.

Torrance, E.P. (1974). Norms-Technical manual: Torrance Tests of creative thinking. Bensenville, IL: Scholastic Testing Service.

Treffinger, D.J. (1986). Research on creativity. *Gifted Child Quarterly*, 30, 15-19.

Tripathi, S.N. (1996). Talent and Creativity. Agra, National Psychological Corporation.

Trotter, R. (1971). Self-image. *Science News*, 100, 130-131.

Tsuin-Chen, O. (1961). Some facts and ideas about talent and genius in chinese history. In G.Z.F. Breday and J.A. Lauwerys (Eds.), Concepts of excellence in education: The yearbook of education. New York: Harcourt, Brace and World.

Vallerand, R.J., Gagne, F., Senecal, C. and Pelletier, L.G. (1994). A comparison of the school intrinsic motivation and perceived competence of gifted and regular students. *Gifted Child Quarterly*, 38(4), 172-175.

Van Tassel-Baska, J. (1998). *Excellence in Educating Gifted and Talented Learners*. Denver, Co: Love Publishing Company.

VanTassel-Baska, J. (1989). Counselling the gifted. In J. Feldhusen, J. Van Tassel-Baska, and K. Seely (Eds.), *Excellence in Educating the Gifted* (pp. 229-314). Denver: Love.

Vasconcellor, J. (1990). Toward a state of esteem. Sacramento: Office of State Printing.

Wallach, M. (1970). Creativity. In. P. Mussen (Ed.), Carmichael's manual of child psychology: Vol.1 (3rd ed.). New York: John Wiley & Sons.

Wallach, M.A. (1985). Creativity testing and giftedness. In F.D. Horowitz and

M.O' Brien (Eds.) The gifted and talented: Developmental perspectives (pp. 99-123). Washington, DC: American Psychological Association.

Wallas, G. (1926). The art of thought. In P.E. Vernon (Ed.) Creativity, Penguin Education, 1970, pp. 91-97.

Walton, G. (1961). Identification of the intellectually gifted children in the public school kindergarten. Unpublished doctoral dissertation, University of California.

Webb, J.T. (1994). Nurturing the social emotional development of gifted children. (Report N. EDOEC-93-10). Reston. VA: Council for Exceptional Children.

Wechsler, D. (1958). The measurement and appraisal of adult intelligence. (4th ed.). Baltimore: Williams and Wilkins.

Wedemeyer, C.A. (1953). Gifted achievers and non-achievers. *Journal of Higher Education*, 24, January, pp. 25-30.

Wells Alan (2005). In parenting: importance of talk by Joanna Moorhead, *The Hindu*, 27 January.

Westcott, M.R. (1961). On the measurement of intuitive leaps. *Psychol. Rep.*, 9, 267-274.

White, W.L. and Renzulli, J.S. (1987). A forty year follow-up of students who attended Leta Hollingworth's school of gifted students. *Roeper Review*, 10, 89-94.

Whitmore, J. (1981). Gifted children with handicapping conditions: A new frontier. *Exceptional Children*, 48, 106-114.

Whitmore, J. and Maker, C.J. (1985). Intellectual giftedness in disabled persons. Denver; Aspen Press.

Whitmore, J.R. (1980). Giftedness, conflict, and under-achievement. Boston: Allyn & Bacon.

Whitmore, J.R. (1986). Understanding a lack of motivation to excel. *Gifted Child Quarterly*, 30, 66-69.

William, H.B., *et. al.* (1951). In P.A. Witty (ed.), Identifying gifted children. The Gifted Child. Boston: D.C. Heath and Co.

Wilson, R. (1957). Improving criteria for complex mental processes. In A.E. Troxler (Ed.). Improving the quality and scope of measurement. Princeton, N.J.: Educational Testing Service.

Witty, P.A. (1930). A study of one hundred gifted children. Bulletin of Education, University of Kansas, Vol. 2, No. 7, Lawrence, Kansas: University of Kansas, February, p. 38.

Witty, P.A. (1940). A genetic study of fifty gifted children. In G.M. Whipple (Ed.), The 39th Yearbook of the National Society for the Study of Education, Part II, Chicago: University of Chicago Press.

Witty, P.A. (1958). "Who are gifted"? In N.D. Henry (Ed.), Education for the gifted: Yearbook of the National Society for the Study of Education, 57, Part 2.

Witty, P.A. and Lehman, H.C. (1929a). Religious leadership and stability. *The psychological Review*, Vol. 36, 1, January, p. 80.

Witty, P.A. and Lehman, H.C. (1929b). Nervous instability and genius. *Journal of Abnormal and Social Psychology*, April-June, p. 78.

Worcester, D.A. (1956). The education of children of above average mental ability. Lincoln, Nebraska: University of Nerbraska Press.

www.geocities.com/Athens/crete/1019/Interests/Potential.html.

www.gogtc.org.au/definitions_of_giftedness.html

www.ibe.unesco.org/international/databanks/Dossiers/ iindia.htm accessed on 28/6/05.

www.ncert.nic.in accessed on 28/6/05.

Zigler, E. and Farber, E.A. (1985). Commonalities between the intellectual extremes: Giftedness and mental retardation. In F.D. Horowitz and M.O' Brien (Eds.), The gifted and talented: Developmental perspectives (pp. 378-408). Washington, DC: American Psychological Association.

Index